The Dao of Civilization

The Dao of Civilization
A Letter to China

Freya Mathews

ANTHEM PRESS

Anthem Press
An imprint of Wimbledon Publishing Company
www.anthempress.com

This edition first published in UK and USA 2023
by ANTHEM PRESS
75–76 Blackfriars Road, London SE1 8HA, UK
or PO Box 9779, London SW19 7ZG, UK
and
244 Madison Ave #116, New York, NY 10016, USA

British Library Cataloguing-in-Publication Data
A catalogue record for this book is available from the British Library.

Library of Congress Control Number: 2022919594
A catalog record for this book has been requested.

ISBN-13: 978-1-83998-485-3 (Pbk)
ISBN-10: 1-83998-485-6 (Pbk)

Cover Image: Detail from Yang Yongliang, Artificial Wonderland, 2010.
Permission kindly granted by the artist.

This title is also available as an e-book.

CONTENTS

Part I

A PHILOSOPHER'S LETTER TO PRESIDENT XI JINPING: ON THE MEANING OF GREATNESS

Dear President Xi Jinping,

I write to you in deep sorrow at the tension that presently clouds the relationship between our two nations. I write as a private Australian citizen, one with no connection to government or political life, but also as a philosopher who has for many years cherished and championed Chinese tradition as a potential source of moral guidance for the modern world, particularly for the West.

In my search for clues as to how modern civilization might reshape itself in response to the unprecedented environmental dangers that now in the twenty-first century threaten our world, I have consistently drawn on the indigenous philosophy of China, Daoism. It is thus in the spirit of all those obscure, mountain-dwelling Daoist recluses to whom Chinese emperors of old occasionally resorted, and whom I hold in such fond regard, that I venture to write to you today.

Your nation, already spectacularly resurgent, makes no secret of the fact that it is striving to become not merely a great superpower, which it manifestly already is, but the greatest, economically overtaking the United States and resuming its historical status as the Middle Kingdom, centre of world civilization.

What might this mean for a small country like Australia? It depends, I think, on the intended meaning of *greatness*. What is greatness, in a nation, an empire, a civilization? Certainly, it is not a matter merely of brute force, the capacity of one nation to coerce other, weaker nations to do its bidding on pain of economic and perhaps other forms of annihilation. Yet this wolfish posture is one that China seems recently to have embraced in relation to

Australia and other countries: do our bidding, Chinese officials seem to say, or we will crush you – we will cripple your economy.

Admittedly Australia has, over the past several decades, been foolishly short-sighted in allowing itself to become economically dependent on trade with China. But China's new punitive demeanour towards Australia serves only to turn us away, driving us to seek alternative markets, other partners. The example China is presently making of Australia sends a shudder of fear but also of revulsion through many countries. If China perseveres in this coercive style, it may lead ultimately to its isolation, at best to a Soviet Union style 'power bloc', a 'bloc' of subordinate nations held together either by brute force or by indentured servitude rather than by loyalty or affinity. In such a bloc, each nation is merely waiting to break free as soon as the iron fist of its oppressor loses its grip. A bloc is not a civilization. There never was a Soviet civilization, for instance. Nor would the Third Reich ever have constituted a civilization, even had Germany won the Second World War. Yet greatness in a nation, I would suggest, is indeed evidenced in *the birth of a new civilization*, in the spontaneous uptake and spread of that civilization across the nation's immediate sphere of influence and beyond.

While such a new civilization cannot be generated merely by force, nor can it result merely from economic inducements, from one nation's offering other nations bald economic incentives to accept its rule – even when those incentives are on the scale of the Belt and Road Initiative. Economic incentives and investments are admittedly effective up to a point, but as soon as a client nation perceives its sovereignty to be at risk from economic indebtedness, resentment and resistance rapidly set in; loyalty is lost. This is what has happened in Australia recently.

What makes for true greatness, the greatness that emanates in a distinctive civilizational flowering, is surely a different kind of power – the power of *attractiveness*. A great power must indeed have military and economic might, but in order to be truly great it must not coerce but *attract* other nations into its orbit. Such a capacity to attract is of course known in diplomatic circles as *soft power*. But soft power is generally understood as a calculated matter of *intent* and *strategy* – it comprises interventions in foreign affairs that are deliberately designed to court the international community. Examples of such interventions perhaps include the BBC's World Service and China's network of Confucius Institutes.

True greatness may reside in something a little different from such merely strategic measures, however shrewd. I would suggest that it emanates from the way a nation influences others by its own example. We could call this a moral example, but it is not quite that either, though it will surely ultimately align with morality. The great nation influences others by means of its capacity to open up new registers of self-actualization in its own society, in its own people, registers of self-actualization that have hitherto been lacking in the world. These new possibilities of self-actualization are such that when other nations witness them, they want them for themselves.

Even Europe in the nineteenth century, though resorting brutally to force in order to colonize large swathes of the world, brought something new to its colonies, something that could not fail to intrigue since it spoke to human potential, to new dimensions and possibilities of human experience, in the form of science and the idea of liberalism – the great shaping ideas that emerged from the European Enlightenment. In the very midst of oppressing its colonies and ruthlessly extracting wealth from their populations and resources, Europe also held out something that had never existed in the world before. Both science and the ideal of individual freedom demonstrably opened up entirely new registers of human self-actualization.

For all the ambivalence that colonized societies felt about their own colonial histories, many of the nations that emerged post the period of European colonization embraced these new possibilities, in part or in whole, of their own accord, in a process that became known as modernization. This is as true of China as it is of so many other non-European nations.

The United States of America affords another example of greatness in this sense, the sense that I would call true greatness. America's status as a superpower in the decades after the Second World War unquestionably rested on military and economic might, might which the United States has unfortunately not been above deploying in unwise, underhanded and otherwise abusive ways outside its own borders.

But military and economic power were by no means alone the key to America's status. It was American culture, unrivalled in its *attractiveness*, that entitled America to claim true greatness in the post-War decades. America's cultural influence was not merely a strategic ploy devised by US agencies to appeal to other nations. This influence was rather the effect that America's own culture, the culture that Americans created for themselves and that defined them as Americans, had on people looking in from the outside. Here was something that those people outside, exhausted by violence and horror after the Second World War, could take to heart – a mood of exuberance, a spirit of generosity and openness to external cultural influences, a sparkling verve that reached out particularly to youth all around the world, via popular music, cinema, media, even industry and technology, drawing people in magnetically.

In the sheer vibrancy of this new culture, people *en masse* sensed fresh and exciting possibilities for self-actualization. Certainly, America exported its music, movies and so on, but it did not create its music industry, its movie industry, for export. The movies and music were in every sense home-grown. Yet for many societies, the American example was irresistible. 'Selling' it was barely required. It was a gift, one that other people already wanted for themselves. There was in the vibrancy and openness of this culture a visceral sense of *freedom*, of unrepressed self-expression, that lent veracity to America's more ideological posture as chief defender of freedom and justice in the world. It was surely only on account of this – its authentic gift to the world – that America's use of its ideological posture to justify the exercise of its military might in a succession of disastrous regional wars was tolerated.

Under the spell of the American example, 'Western' civilization, with its origins in Europe on foundations of science and liberalism and its nineteenth-century Anglicization by means of the British Empire, became substantially Americanized. In this form the US has wielded a new and pervasive civilizational influence globally, albeit selectively and of course not without significant push-back. It is surely via this civilizational influence that it has earned its title to greatness.

Recently, however, as we are all well aware, this title to greatness has been unravelling. The grief and confusion that many Americans have in consequence experienced enabled political opportunists like Donald Trump to distort the nature of that erstwhile greatness. The 'greatness' that Trump invoked through his slogan, 'Make America Great Again', was mere grandiosity and brute power, a power to be regained by exchanging the spirit that made America so attractive – its openness and generosity – for a surly hostility and stance of superiority to the outside world. Manifestly no longer a defender of freedom and justice either at home or abroad, the United States became, in the Trump era, America the Heartless, persecutor of refugees; America the Unjust, home of white supremacy; America the Faithless, betrayer of allies. America, land of the free, degenerated into America, land of the merely unruly, land of deniers of self-evident truths, whether pertaining to pandemics, climate change or the outcome of an election.

In the mass psychosis unleashed by these reversals of its legitimate claims to greatness – a psychosis surreally acted out in the historic storming of the Capitol at the beginning of 2021 – we can see that greatness is not merely a matter of rhetoric, but emanates from a genuine spiritual core with which a nation loses touch at its peril.

So, what are the new possibilities for self-actualization that China might, through its own example, offer to the world in this era of upheaval on so many fronts? Now that science and liberalism are wearing thin as an exclusive axis for civilization, even in the West itself, and many nations are beginning to turn away from modernity as a marker of identity, back towards their own historical traditions – traditions that may nonetheless be of limited relevance in face of the unprecedented challenges of the twenty-first century – what new possibilities might China exemplify? What is currently most lacking in our collective capacity as humans to adapt civilization to the needs of our time?

The answer would be clear, I think, to any Daoist sage wandering down from his or her mountain fastness into the choking fumes, the leafless concrete canyons, of any modern city. They would see modern society as having departed – drastically, shockingly – from *Dao*.

Dao, as I do not need to explain to you, is the great *Way*, the way that the world spontaneously regenerates itself when the Ten Thousand Things actualize themselves in concert with, rather than in opposition to, one another. It is the self-replenishing wellspring of new form when new form arises from never-ending processes of mutual accommodation amongst the old. Mutual accommodation is the Daoist key to cosmic regeneration. But modernity is premised on the opposite of this. Modernity is premised not on synergy with nature but on techno-mastery thereof. This mindset of techno-mastery, which has now resulted in domination and destruction of Earth-life on a planetary scale, is rooted directly in an assumption of human/nature dualism that lies at the very root of the Western tradition.

Because this dualistic mindset – which splits mind from matter, culture from nature, observer from observed, subject from object, atom from atom, fact from value – is endemic to the Western imagination, from whence it has been exported to the world at large by means of modernization, the remedy for it does not lie in Western thought. But *Dao*, which is the very taproot of Chinese civilization, as alive and formative in the workings of the Chinese mind today as it ever was, knows no such divide. It is because *Dao*, albeit invisibly, continues to shape the Chinese imagination that China exhibits its characteristic syncretic tendencies, its pragmatic disposition to accommodate new ideas as they present rather than contend with them, or suffer contention amongst them. It was surely this same Daoist mindset that enabled China to recruit Western science and technology, and implement modernization, when the challenge arose, adapting itself to these new modes of self-actualization.

But a danger has lurked in this latest phase of Chinese syncretism. In opening itself to science, and the project of techno-mastery that accompanies it, China risks killing the living shoot of *Dao* that has nourished its own openness, its *wuwei* readiness to adapt and absorb, where this *wuwei* readiness has surely been the secret of China's longevity. Science, taken not merely as one knowledge-tool amongst others but as the very measure of reality, insists on its own truth and thereby overrides the gentle syncretism of *Dao*.

This killing of *Dao* as wellspring of Chinese civilization must not be allowed to occur. *Dao* can be retrieved, rescued from its present state of relative cultural oversight in China. Reinstated to its rightful place as root and guide, it can fully revision existing modes of production so that they, and the entire social and economic infrastructure they undergird, including manufacture, architecture and agriculture, become compatible with the needs of the biosphere.

Many intimations of such a new paradigm of production are already to hand. In agriculture, philosophies such as those of permaculture, ecological agriculture, restorative agriculture, natural sequence farming, extensive as opposed to intensive farming, not to mention the older farming traditions of China itself, all represent ecologically oriented challenges to modern modes of agribusiness. In manufacturing, regenerative design philosophies are pointing the way towards methods that work with the grain of natural systems rather than against them.

But the detailed, creative application of explicitly *Daoist* principles across these fields promises a design revolution such as has not been witnessed since the first Industrial Revolution in the West. By thinking in this mode, which is the special province of Chinese culture, humanity could again find, as in olden days, synergy and synchrony with the natural environment. Ultimately, if applied to politics and international relations as well, synergy and synchrony amongst peoples and societies might also eventuate.

Such an ecological revision of the foundations of society might not at this moment appear to be a top priority for millions of Chinese still seeking prosperity through 'modern' modes of industrialization that originated in the West. But it will speak directly to the longings and anxieties of young people around the world: such a capacity for ecological imagination is what their own societies most deeply lack. If China can develop ecological modes of self-actualization amongst its own populace by adapting Daoist thought to the context of climate change, mass extinctions, global pollution and ecosystem collapse, then young people the world over will eagerly follow the Chinese example, and a new eco-Daoist civilization will spontaneously spread. China's greatness will be warmly acknowledged and embraced.

Amongst its own people, the pride in national identity that is presently taking alienating, wolfish and surely ultimately self-defeating forms will be reinvested in the new, eco-Daoist modes of self-actualization that will by then have become widely acclaimed and taken up around the world. With such reinvestment, Chinese people might indeed become ready to give ecological goals precedence over other priorities.

The fate of the biosphere is bound up with the way China chooses to design its continued industrial rise in the twenty-first century. Happily, China has, uniquely, at the very roots of its own tradition, the philosophical resources to meet this unprecedented challenge. It can devise authentic forms of civilization that the world desperately needs and that younger generations worldwide desperately want. If China can meet this need, such younger generations will not hesitate to become *Sinicized*, to make these forms of civilization their own, just as earlier generations of young people did not hesitate to become Americanized. China will be acknowledged again as the Middle Kingdom, not out of fear or servility but out of gratitude. And the only wolves in sight will be those that will have returned to their mountainous home ranges to live in peace amongst the Daoist sages.

May China indeed achieve its true and proper greatness. Such greatness will not of course set it above criticism. Greatness brings great challenges, great responsibilities and hence great risks of error: the great nation therefore depends upon its critics to alert it to mistakes. But it may expect such criticism to be delivered with supreme courtesy and tact, with a respect commensurate with the degree to which its influence has enlarged the world. True greatness effortlessly earns such respect.

With deepest sincerity and faith in Chinese integrity,

Freya Mathews/Ma Feiya

Part II

BY THE LAW OF THE LIVING COSMOS: SHANGHAI LECTURES ON ECOLOGICAL CIVILIZATION

INTRODUCTION

I arrived in Shanghai in July 2019 to deliver a series of lectures in the Sino-British Summer School of Philosophy, a venerable annual event that began in the 1980s and is organized jointly by the Chinese Academy of Social Sciences and the Royal Institute of Philosophy in the UK. In 2019 the Summer School was held in the East China Normal University and its topic was Environmental Philosophy. I had agreed to participate on the understanding that my lectures would present strands of thinking about ecological civilization that I had been developing in a series of papers over many years. I was keen to try these ideas out with a group of Chinese students before condensing them into book form. Those lectures, duly written up, enlarged and updated, are the ones I offer here.

The stint at the Summer School was not my first trip to China. I had visited many times over the previous 15 years, attending conferences and workshops in environmental ethics as well as studying the traditional Daoist arts of *taiji* and *neidan* (internal alchemy) with various teachers on mountains and in temples. I seemed to have some 'business' in China. Invitations, often from unrelated parties, tended to arrive out of the blue. Overseas travel generally is not my forte; I have neither the constitution for it nor the keen professionalism that thrusts academics onto the international conference circuit – or at least did so until the Covid pandemic changed all that. I actually have no desire to leave Australia, or even the precincts of my own little stone mountain in my home state of Victoria. Like a good Daoist, I relish my seclusion. But China kept tugging at me, in a way that so touched my heart that I could not help but answer its call, though this forced me back into the punishing scenarios of vast airports and transport hubs – into states of alienation from all that I hold dear.

There is no mystical denouement to this story. My three weeks spent walking from the staff hotel to our classrooms on the modern, spacious campus of the East China Normal University did not change my life, any more than my earlier, more picturesque sojourns in the Wudang and Emei Mountains or my pilgrimage to the utterly numinous Queen of all Chinese mountains, Tai Shan, had done. Life is neither a fairy tale nor a mystical Daoist romance.

But there are, arguably, poetic patterns, patterns of meaning that may be discerned beneath the often-chequered ordinariness of everyday affairs; one might choose either to ignore them or align with them. If one aligns with them, the contours of those larger, hidden, poetic patterns may become a little more discernible. That is all.

So the dinners and lunches spent in convivial debate with my colleagues in Shanghai – Xiao Laoshi (Xiao Yang), En Laoshi (William Edelglass), Shi Laoshi (Colette Sciberras) and Yu Laoshi (Yu Feng) – and the many hours spent exchanging philosophical perspectives with charming younger and older students of varying backgrounds from all over China drew me somehow into an invisible pattern that, a year or so later, emanated in my Letter, already presented here in Part I, 'A Philosopher's Letter to President Xi Jinping'. The freshness, fondness and deep courtesy of those students – the way many of them opened their hearts to their foreign teachers – dissolved the boundaries between our worlds, at least to the point where I felt, at some subterranean level, that their Leader was not beyond my reach. He belonged now not only to their moral universe but to mine.

I was also interested to learn from the students that in China political leaders are not entirely unwilling to consort with philosophers. What a contrast with the situation in the West! In liberal democracies, unlike in China, philosophers are free to talk to the people, in the sense of trying to influence public opinion, though the people, captive to corporate interests incessantly legislated by government, have little inclination to listen. But the doors of political leaders, beholden to those corporate interests, are firmly closed to critical thinkers. Politics is effectively in this way, in the liberal democracies of the West, segregated from critical thinking. Critical thinking is relegated to the academy, and the academy is left pretty much talking to itself. In China, on the other hand, while philosophers are not free to talk to the people, in the sense that there is little tolerance for street-level movements for social change, there are established channels – think tanks and consultative committees – whereby those in the academy are invited to advise on policy. Leaders are, in other words, not closed to new ideas, and may even seek them out, like rulers of old calling respectable Confucians or wandering Daoists to the court of the emperor, when it is felt that a philosophical change of direction is needed. It was this information that emboldened me to append my Shanghai Lectures to my Letter to the Supreme Leader.

As my interlude in Shanghai drew to a close, there was, as it happened, an arresting coda. The Summer School ended earlier than I had expected and for a couple of days I was left with nothing to do. I waited fretfully for my scheduled flight. But when the day of departure arrived, a typhoon of extreme ferocity made landfall south of Shanghai and bore down on the city. Early that evening, as my taxi sped towards the airport, the freeways were already awash. Through the window I watched as we passed dim, hunched figures on feeble unlit motor scooters battling to get home with heavy loads, their flapping water-proofs affording them no protection at all. At the side of the freeway there was no safety lane or verge, just a concrete wall. One of these – unhelmeted – figures was walking his scooter, which must have broken down; cars streamed past him in the near-dark, missing him by inches.

Pudong airport, when I arrived, was pandemonium. Flights were being cancelled on every side. My flight was still on schedule, and so it remained until after midnight, when the plane simply failed to show up from Japan. Throughout this time there were no announcements. The staff of China East Airlines knew nothing; they refused – extremely rudely – to answer inquiries, looking away or shouting at passengers. Suddenly no one seemed to speak English and on overhead screens any information about flight schedules was in Chinese only. There were no more than a handful of foreigners in evidence around the China East Airlines desks. By dint of continual pestering of people around me I managed to get myself successively to the right departure gates. All night our flight continued to be 'delayed', while almost all others were cancelled. More than a thousand flights into and out of Shanghai were cancelled that night. Only ours and a couple of others were, for some inscrutable reason, delayed rather than cancelled. So, we waited, camped around closed doors on the floor, without food, since the airport had almost completely shut down. 'Service' was non-existent and distinctions between first class and economy class had long since become meaningless. Before dawn China East did distribute water bottles and sandwiches to remaining passengers so that we would survive. Finally, the following afternoon, our plane arrived. At around 2.00 pm we were asked to board. There had been no airport announcements of any kind for 15 hours.

Our plane, setting out towards its airstrip, seemed to be the only one left in the deserted expanses of Pudong. The long grass between the many runways was blowing flat and rippling uncannily fast like frantic water. Rivers of rain streamed across endless expanses of tarmac. Taxi-ing hesitantly, the plane found its allocated runway, turned and, pointing its nose directly into the gale, revved itself up, gathering its power and girding its loins. Then it plunged recklessly into that gale. Suspended in a prolonged moment of uncertainty, I felt a strange exhilaration rather than fear. Then there was lift-off, albeit in bucking bronco style, and very soon we were high above the tumult.

Surely this coda to my time in Shanghai was a preview of our new climate-distressed world: all our conveniences, our schedules, our technological mastery, our confident constructs, reduced overnight to a shambles, if not to rubble. Did my heart exult for that moment as I looked out at the wind-and-water dragons sweeping the vast airport clean – clear of our clutter – because I was witnessing the planet effortlessly taking back its own?

Lecture 1

WHAT IS WRONG WITH THE WESTERN WORLDVIEW? IS DUALISM THE PROBLEM?

Early Days of Environmental Philosophy: the Problem of Dualism

In the 1970s–1980s a radical critique of traditional Western approaches to nature emerged simultaneously at various flashpoints in the Western world, notably Australia, Norway and the USA.

The Norwegian critique emanated from philosopher Arne Naess who became the founder of the deep ecology movement. In the USA a handful of emerging philosophers, amongst them Holmes Rolston, Baird Callicott and Eugene Hargrove, gave voice to their environmental concerns in a new journal, *Environmental Ethics*. There was a less well-known but just as trenchant Australian critique from the Routleys (later known as Richard Sylvan and Val Plumwood) at the Australian National University. All these early philosophers recognized that the environmental problems that were coming into view at that time were the result not merely of faulty policies and technologies but of underlying attitudes to the natural world that were built into the very foundations of Western thought.

For all of them, the notion of *anthropocentrism* was key to these attitudes. Anthropocentrism was the groundless belief, amounting to nothing more than prejudice, that only human beings matter, morally speaking; to the extent that anything else – animals, plants, ecosystems, the natural world generally – matters, it does so only because it has some kind of utility for human beings. Together, these early philosophers challenged this assumption and asked, as Richard Routley put it in his 1973 paper of the same name, 'is there a need for a new, an environmental, ethic?'. By an environmental ethic they meant an ethic of nature, an ethic that treats nature as morally considerable in its own right.

This early challenge to anthropocentrism set the agenda for the new discipline of environmental philosophy, which proceeded to mature through the 1980s and 1990s as a new generation of thinkers joined the inquiry.

Why, these philosophers wondered, had the West developed such a blinding moral prejudice against nature and in favour of humanity? It was clear that some kind of *dualism* or *binarism* was at work – a dichotomizing tendency that set the human apart from and above nature. The human stood as the measure of all meaning and value against the brute facticity of nature. Why? What was so special about the human?

The Roots of the Dualistic Conception of Matter and Mind in Classical Science

In due course many environmental philosophers converged on an answer: the special attribute that was perceived as setting humans apart from the rest of nature was *mind*. Without mental attributes of some description, an entity cannot matter to itself or in itself since it cannot have meaning, value, interests or ends of its own. Only a being that matters to itself, that seeks its own good or pursues ends of its own, can have intrinsic moral, as opposed to merely instrumental, significance: if a thing does not matter to itself, why would it matter what we do to it, except insofar as what we do might have consequences for other beings that do matter to themselves? If humans alone possess mind, then humans alone matter to themselves and are hence alone entitled to moral consideration. But why assume that humans alone possess mind and that the rest of nature is blank and blind?

In searching for an answer to this question, environmental philosophers often blamed the mechanistic view of matter that the West had inherited from the Galilean-Newtonian science of the seventeenth century (Easlea 1973; Merchant 1980; Berman 1981; Mathews 1991). This is now a familiar refrain in environmental literature, but just briefly to recap: from the mechanistic viewpoint, nature can be exhaustively described and explained in materialist terms. Nature is matter, where matter in itself is, from this perspective, sheer externality – there is nothing in it that is not empirically observable, or observable from the outside. There are no indwelling powers or agencies that cannot be fully accounted for in terms of regular or lawlike patterns of external motion imparted by external forces. (Gravitation was admittedly for Newton an anomaly in this respect; as such, he saw it as an 'occult' phenomenon, not quite integrated into science.) Macro-level material objects or bodies are merely aggregations of particles that are likewise fully externalized and inert, moved and arranged in accordance with external laws.

Our own experience of ourselves as subjectival beings, moved from within by inner, inherent impulses not observable from the outside, stands in contrast to such reductive materialism. We cannot doubt that aspects of our behaviour emanate from a mysterious 'inner life' that is invisible to others. This inner, felt dimension seems then to divide us from the world of mere matter. According to Descartes, this inner dimension is indeed the primary datum: we can doubt the very existence of the external world, the world of mere matter, but we cannot doubt our inner world, since in the very act of doubting it we testify to its existence – *cogito ergo sum*. This is the basis of Descartes' famous mind-matter dualism. But at the same time *only* humans can demonstrate their mental existence in this declarative manner. Since explanation of the observed behaviour of all other, non-human living things seems in principle conceivable in Newtonian terms, mind winds up, in this Cartesian frame of reference, as exclusively the province of humans.

The origins of dualism may arguably be traced much further back than the seventeenth century – all the way back to the origins of Western civilization in ancient Greece and early Christianity (White 1967; Oelschlaeger 1991; Plumwood 1993). Indeed, I shall suggest later that dualism is ultimately rooted in the agrarian revolution that took place in the Neolithic (Mathews 2019b). But the Scientific Revolution unquestionably represents the historical moment in which mind-matter dualism came into its sharpest philosophical focus.

The Environmental Challenge to the Dualistic Conception of Mind and Matter

But surely, environmental philosophers protested, such a black-and-white dualism of mind and matter, that reserves mind for humans and represents the rest of nature as literally mindless and hence devoid of meaning, purpose and moral status of its own, is simply wrong? From the 1980s, and over the next three decades, the race was on to expand the conception of mind and discover mental attributes, in some larger than Cartesian sense, in nature – thereby extending the scope of moral significance beyond the human.

This inquiry of course raised a plethora of questions without clear-cut answers. What was 'mind' in this larger sense? Did it necessarily entail consciousness or subjectivity? Who or what was imbued with it? Living things? But what counts as a living thing? Do individual organisms alone count as living things, or do larger living systems count as well? Should an environmental ethic cover *all* living things? Should plants and fungi count as morally considerable in their own right? If so, how considerable? As considerable as animals? Should a distinction be made, morally speaking, between higher and lower animals? But which animals are higher and which lower? And what about microbes? Single cells? Viruses? Species? And natural features of the landscape that are not alive, such as rocks and rivers? Is the entire landscape, or Earth itself, a living thing? Or indeed, is the universe as a whole alive? And again, might we regard the landscape, Earth or the entire universe as alive without ascribing mind to it?

Environmental philosophers of course disagreed with one another in their answers to these questions. Some even argued that it was not necessary to challenge anthropocentrism (nor hence dualism) at all in order to extend adequate protection to the natural environment: instrumentalism – the view that the environment is only meaningfully valuable as a resource for human use – might afford a sufficient basis for environmental protection if we as humans conserve our natural resource base wisely and well. Other environmental philosophers argued that though nature might indeed be regarded as intrinsically valuable and therefore as morally considerable in its own right, this was for other reasons than that it was imbued with mind; it might be because it was beautiful, for example, or was God's Creation.

But most environmental philosophers of this period did seek to extend moral considerability to the natural environment on the grounds that it was at least in part imbued, like humans, with mental attributes, in some larger sense of 'mental' that nevertheless implied that it possessed interests or ends of its own that in turn conferred self-mattering and self-meaning. (For a round-up of the various arguments for and against the intrinsic value and consequent moral considerability of the natural world, see Brennan and Lo 2021.)

How to Dismantle Dualism

It was widely agreed then that dualism was the problem and hence that the solution must lie in overcoming dualism. But how was this to be achieved? Would overcoming dualism consist simply of putting back together again what dualism had sundered – restoring mind, under some new or larger description, to matter?

Seeking to address this question in the late twentieth century required coming to terms with shifts that had occurred in the configuration of dualism since the seventeenth century. In the absence of significant physiological perspectives on mental function at that time, Descartes had posited mind as a mysterious, God-given, metaphysical 'substance' in its own right, categorically distinct from matter and exclusively the province of humans. By the twentieth century, however, increasingly sophisticated physiological – neurological – accounts of mental function were available, and the Cartesian assumption of mind as a distinct metaphysical 'substance' no longer had currency outside minority philosophical (and perhaps religious) circles. Rather, by this time, mind was regarded as a – still admittedly mysterious – correlate of certain specialized physical – neurological – structures. Matter was thus considered as ontologically primary; mind, though still special, was considered derivative. This reduction of mind to matter was generally referred to as materialism.

While the triumph of materialism might look like the collapse of mind-matter dualism in favour of matter monism, it in fact perpetuated dualism in its very conception of matter. Matter in its essential nature was defined in terms of its systematic exclusion of all qualities associated with mentality, such as subjectivity, agency, purpose, meaning and intentionality. In other words, matter was defined in opposition to mind, and in that respect its definition perpetuated, in a ghostly, relict form, the very dualism it purported to deny. At the same time, humans were still, even in the twentieth century, widely regarded as the exclusive possessors of the specialized neurological equipment required for full consciousness. In this sense, the old anthropocentrism that had accompanied the original Newtonian-Cartesian version of dualism persisted through the transition to late twentieth-century materialism.

In the latter part of the twentieth century, some philosophers had already taken a step towards challenging anthropocentrism by attributing full consciousness, and hence moral considerability, to a range of non-human animals (Singer 1975; Tom Regan 1983). This position has recently received resounding validation from science itself: leading neuro-scientists have acknowledged that many species of animals share with humans the basic neurological substrates that generate consciousness. Neurology pertaining to emotions, for example, is found across a wide range of species; animals who are neurologically wired in this way must, many scientists now insist, experience the same emotions and associated states of consciousness – including fear, terror, jealousy and grief – as do humans.[1] Even entomologists, such as eminent conservation scientist E. O. Wilson, describe certain species of ants and bees as literally learning from experience and making decisions (Wilson 2009).

In the early twenty-first century, an array of philosophers and botanists have gone so far as to ascribe mind, or at any rate mind-like properties, to plants and perhaps to fungi: in forests, for example, trees communicate with one another via electrical and chemical signals transmitted through underground mycorrhizal (fungal) networks (the 'wood-wide web') (Wohlleben 2015; Hall 2011). Through such networks, mature, healthy trees also deliver nutrients and water to trees in need and neighbouring trees can be warned of insect attacks. In experiments, botanist Monica Gagliano has shown that plants can 'learn' to distinguish between relevant and irrelevant stimuli and

---

1 See the 2012 Cambridge Declaration on Consciousness. http://fcmconference.org/img/CambridgeDeclarationOnConsciousness.pdf Accessed 8 January 2020.

will 'remember' what they have learned for extended periods (Pollan 2013). Although there is by no means agreement amongst botanists as to the interpretation of these experimental findings, the findings themselves are being widely discussed. In consequence, many people, at least in the West, now indeed seem prepared to countenance the idea that animals, plants and perhaps fungi are forms of life endowed with degrees of intelligence, sentience or consciousness. The further inference that such beings are entitled to a degree of moral consideration in their own right is likewise increasingly widespread.

Though this undoubtedly represents a major advance over the strict anthropocentrism that was still prevalent in both science and Western society only a generation or two ago, such new inclusiveness scarcely amounts to a thoroughgoing dismantling of dualism. All the scientific debate around mind in animals, plants and other forms of life shares what might be described as the neurocentric assumption: mind emanates exclusively from neurological structures or physiological analogues thereof. Such a neurocentric approach leaves in place the metaphysical assumption that matter is, at the most fundamental level, inherently insentient, dead and blind. Instances of emergent mind exist only as a scatter of tiny islands of self-transparency in an otherwise dark, self-indifferent and intrinsically meaningless universe. The ground we walk, the sky overhead, the stars above are still dead matter, in themselves sheer externality, and accordingly there for us to use as we see fit. Selectively including animals and other organisms in the circle of the mentally endowed – and hence morally elect – amounts only to an extension of the logic that underlies anthropocentrism.

Truly to reorient ourselves to reality, however, to walk with a gentler step that betokens true escape from the dualist mind-set, with its default instrumentalism, we might need to open the category of mind up to wider-than-neurological interpretations.

Relational and Distributive Approaches to Dismantling Dualism: Mind without Consciousness

Some environmental philosophers, refusing to settle for the neurocentric approach, did indeed seek to open the category of mind up to larger-than-neurological interpretations. Typically, such approaches relied on relational or distributive perspectives: mind was construed as inhering in the relational aspect of larger systems as a distributive property of those systems, rather than as emanating exclusively from a neurological core or cores. The paradigm example of such a system is perhaps the ecosystem: individual organisms belonging to a given ecosystem may prima facie possess specific degrees of intelligence but, from a relational perspective, the system itself also possesses its own pervasive – distributive – intelligence in which all its members share. So, for example, while the Blue Whale is known to be a creature of prodigious intelligence, capable of complex communication across astonishing distances, it has functionally evolved to feed on tiny krill. Its entire anatomy – in particular, its baleen mouth – embodies a non-contingent reference to krill. In this sense, from an ecological point of view, Blue Whale functionality is internally related to krillian functionality: Blue Whales are not merely causally, but also logically, inextricable from krill. When species identities are viewed relationally in this way, mental attributes cannot be seen as the preserve of just one or a few special species: cetacean intelligence is not the province exclusively of cetaceans but is rather implicated in the ecosystem to which the cetacean in question belongs. In the case of the Blue Whale, it is shared by the humble krill. (Mathews 1991)

This is what founding ecophilosopher Arne Naess meant, back in 1973, when he wrote that the notion of a 'thing in its environment' should be replaced with a 'relational, total-field image'. Organisms should be viewed not as separate entities in their own right but as 'knots in the biospherical net or field of intrinsic relations' (Naess 1973).

Human identity, according to ecophilosophers of this stripe, is no different from Blue Whale identity. It is constituted through and through by its relations with other species and communities of life. Far from being a 'higher', mentally endowed subject, set apart from and looking down on a 'lower', blind nature, the human self is an *ecological self*, its identity a function of relations with other species and elements of the earth environment (Naess 1985; Fox 1990; Mathews 1991). Mind is implicated in, or distributed throughout, this mesh of relations, and cannot be regarded as the province of a privileged entity.

Another, even earlier variant of this relational, distributive approach to mind in nature is that of Gregory Bateson. According to Bateson, mind is a process that is continuously occurring at every level of living systems, from the cellular to the biospheric. It is intrinsic to the kind of organizational processes whereby living systems interact with one another in order to evolve, differentiate and maintain themselves in existence. Bateson pictures mind not as a 'thing' (as in 'my mind' or 'the mind of a dolphin') that belongs to an entity but as a vast, dispersed, systemic process drawing entities into complex, mutually constituting interactions, while always also opening out into new, nested levels of organization. In this sense, mentality is conceived by him more as verb – as 'thinking' – than as noun. (Bateson 1979; Charlton 2008: 68)

Such adaptive and productive thought processes are, according to Bateson, taking place everywhere in both living systems and society. They encompass systems of interaction amongst human individuals in groups – families, communities, committees, corporations, nations – and amongst the elements of biospherical systems and cycles. While not necessarily conscious, such processes do constitute intelligence. Indeed, biological, ecological and evolutionary processes represent for Bateson the highest orders of intelligence: human reason, so vaunted in the history of Western philosophy, trails far behind the unconscious thought processes even of the human body, let alone the wider processes structuring ecology and evolution.

Variants of the distributive approach have gained currency more recently in the philosophy of mind. According to the 'extended' theory of mind, associated with Andy Clarke and David Chalmers, the environment of an organism – under both its animate and inanimate aspects – plays an active role in driving cognitive processes. In this sense, inanimate objects and technologies, such as computers, as well as mnemonic props of all kinds, including sentient ones, can become integral to 'extended' processes of thinking. Since they shape particular modes of cognition, they may be said to co-create these modes. The claim is not so much that such entities possess mental attributes of their own but that in interaction with organisms they become integral to larger mental pathways or systems. In a comparable vein, the 'enactive' approach to mind, associated particularly with Francisco Varela and Evan Thompson, situates cognition in the interactive space between organism and environment. Salient aspects of the environment draw forth distinctive cognitive capacities. In this sense they are integral to cognition per se: without the activation of such a functional fit between organisms and their environment, mind would not exist. Mind therefore cannot be understood as merely the province of neurology but resides in a nexus of selective interactivity between bodies and their lived worlds. Mind is hence a doing, a meaning-making process that is fully contextualized to environmental niches.

In all these distributive accounts a distinction persists between systems with mental properties and systems without. Boundaries around mental systems have loosened; they have become more porous and contextual than the categorical boundary that separated mind from matter in the old Cartesian scenario. But mind is by no means yet co-extensive with matter. For Bateson, and I think perhaps also for more recent proponents of such distributive approaches, instances of matter that are not caught up with living systems will entirely lack mental properties. The inanimacy and mindlessness of matter antedates the emergence of living systems. Bateson is explicit on this point: he calls the realm of the living, *Creatura*, and that of the non-living, *Pleroma* (Bateson and Bateson 1987).

Although such expanded views of mind take us considerably closer to dismantling mind-matter dualism than did the neurocentric approach, we might still wonder whether, from an environmental perspective, they have taken us far enough. While they might indeed encourage us to comport ourselves more respectfully towards all forms of *biosis*, our default modality will remain the instrumental one: wherever our actions are deemed not to impinge on living systems or the environments to which they are, or may become, adapted, we shall feel free to blast and carve up physical terrain in our habitual manner.

In order genuinely to dismantle dualism, and so reinhabit reality in an entirely new, non-instrumental fashion, let us at least try to take a further step, the step towards a thoroughgoing panpsychism, to see where this leads us.

Introducing Panpsychism

According to the view that I am here calling panpsychism, mind is not merely a correlate of certain neurological structures or neural-structures-in-interaction-with-their-environments but is a fundamental aspect of matter per se. To put it another way, mind is not merely distributed more widely in the living world than Western science traditionally allowed; it is actually intrinsic to matter: there can be no matter that is not also inherently imbued with mind. There is in this sense no 'brute matter', no such thing as the purely externalized 'stuff' proposed by classical physics – no Pleroma.

This is not to say that matter is not in itself real or that it can be reduced to mind. Material objects do not exist merely 'in the mind' of observers, as traditional Idealists argued. Such objects do exist in their own right. But to exist as a material object is at the same to possess a certain inner, fundamentally subjectival aspect that is not reducible to externally observable attributes.

Whether the inner properties thus ascribed to matter are characterized in terms of agency, teleology or intentionality or more overtly psychological properties, such as consciousness, experience, phenomenality or spirit, they cannot be captured in purely *extensional* terms; that is to say, they cannot be described in terms of properties that are fully observable from the outside. In other words, according to panpsychists, materiality per se has a depth dimension, inaccessible to observation, as well as an external, observable dimension. The universe is inwardly textured, as a terrain of subjectivity, as well as outwardly articulated, as matter behaving in accordance with the laws of physics.

Such a view of the nature of reality may be theorized in a variety of very different ways, from W. K. Clifford's 'mind stuff', Whitehead's 'prehending' particles and Williams James' 'mind dust' to the self-active universes of Spinoza, Schelling and David Bohm (Skrbina 2005).

There are several contemporary streams of thought that are either explicitly panpsychist or overlap with panpsychism. The most influential is panpsychism as a theory within the philosophy of mind. Before looking at this, let us briefly note two other discourses that overlap with panpsychism though the term 'panpsychism' is rarely deployed in them. The first of these discourses is the new animism; the second, the so-called 'new materialisms'.

The new animism is generally less a fully fledged philosophical theory than a worldview adapted from pre-existing Indigenous traditions. As leading exponent Graham Harvey puts it, animism is generally understood less as a philosophical explanation of mind in nature than as a metaphysical conviction emanating in a protocol for comporting oneself in a world filled with other-than-human agencies and intelligences (Harvey 2012). In this sense, new animists do not so much argue with science as move into the niche in society traditionally occupied by religion.

The new materialisms arose relatively recently in the context of deconstructive cultural and literary theory and have permeated the discourse of the environmental humanities (Coole and Frost 2010). The deconstructive stance was marked by a pronounced tendency towards epistemological relativism on the grounds that truth-claims about the fundamental nature of things generally serve as ideological tools to naturalize and legitimate political oppression. This was the stance famously described by philosopher Jean-Francois Lyotard as 'incredulity towards meta-narratives'. Such relativism in turn entailed a withdrawal from any kind of common-sense realism with respect to the world. Wariness of realism however proved a fatal handicap in providing political orientation to everyday technological, biological, medical, geographical, environmental and climate realities. As a school then, the new materialism has sought to reconcile its original conviction regarding the proactive role of the knower in the 'construction' of the known with a healthier measure of realism regarding our everyday world. ('New realism' might better describe the import of this discourse than 'new materialism' does, since its aim is to reinstate a non-naïve form of realism which accords a fundamental role to mind in the constitution of reality. To describe the position as a form of materialism is, to say the least, confusing, since 'materialism' has generally been understood in the history of philosophy as a view that denies mind, as a fundamental attribute, to matter.) Since environmental philosophers did not, by and large, share the relativist premise of the deconstructive tradition however, little in the way of dialogue has taken place across the two schools.

The most influential contemporary discourse that is explicitly panpsychist may be found in the philosophy of mind. It tackles current, received scientific – neurological – accounts of consciousness and asks how and why consciousness, as it appears in the history of evolution, could ever have emerged out of brute matter via mere physical processes. As philosopher of consciousness, David Chalmers, pointed out in 1996, organisms could have evolved sophisticated information-processing faculties, together with appropriate responsive capabilities, without ever having become conscious at all (Chalmers 1996). To put this slightly differently, organisms could have developed sensitivities to their environments and the capability for adaptive responses, without becoming subject to any kind of inner activity corresponding to experience: they could have evolved, to use Chalmer's term, as 'zombies'. The panpsychist solution to this zombie problem, a reply variously theorized, is that consciousness never did emerge out of brute matter because no such thing as brute matter ever existed in the first place: matter has always been imbued with some degree of sentience and is so imbued all the way down to the most elementary level.

Arguments for panpsychism in the theory of consciousness generally follow an analytical pattern. By 'analytical' here I mean an approach that seeks to understand a thing by breaking it down into its basic components or constituents. Available terminology is rather thin on the ground in this connection. 'Atomist' is sometimes used to denote an analysis-based approach, but since 'atomist' conjures the (atomic) nature of the constituents themselves rather than merely the method that seeks to arrive at them, I shall generally use the term 'dissective' to refer to this analysis-based method. Dissective or analysis-based arguments for panpsychism adhere closely to the accounts of consciousness offered by neuro-science and evolutionary biology; indeed they tend to share the entire schema of neurological and evolutionary explanation with science, merely adding, at every level of theorization, the rider that the theoretical particles and structures defined at that level must also be ascribed with an undefined mental attribute of their own. While perhaps resolving outright anomalies in materialist accounts of mind, this dissective approach seems to add little to our understanding of mental phenomena, merely stopping up, by metaphysical fiat, an explanatory hole in the science of mind.

Has our inquiry – our quest to 'overcome dualism' in order to correct our state of moral alienation from our world – thus here run into a dead end? With dissective panpsychism, dualism is surely overcome: mind is restored as an intrinsic and irreducible aspect of matter. But the world is still made up of logically 'distinct existences', as the eighteenth-century philosopher David Hume might have put it: entities which, though perhaps causally related to other entities, could nevertheless be conceived in and through themselves. In the case of dissective panpsychism, these entities correspond to particles of various kinds, locked together by laws of physics, but contingently so, since the laws of physics themselves are contingent: they could have been otherwise. Each of these particles may be apportioned a dim glimmer of mind, but such glimmers must be so miniscule as to be of negligible moral significance. Nor is it clear how the mental properties of such particles could be summed in such a way as to amount, in aggregate, to more morally significant instances of mind.

(This is the famous Combination Problem of panpsychism (Chalmers 2016; Skrbina 2005)). Even if they could be so summed, the resulting aggregates – macro-objects endowed with mind – would, from the dissective perspective, themselves constitute 'distinct existences'. As such they would face the problem that has beset Western accounts of morality from the start, namely that they leave unanswered the question, why be moral at all?

Let me pause here to explain. Were we convinced that all material entities were endowed to some degree with mind, we might indeed feel obliged to treat them with consideration in accordance with the strictures of morality. But in a world consisting of distinct existences – which is to say, the world as viewed through a dissective lens – morality ultimately fails to answer its own question, *why be moral*? For anybody endowed with sympathy or sensitivity to the inner life of others, yes, the strictures of morality may feel binding. But for those who happen to lack such sentiments, and on whom no punishment will fall if they fail to obey those strictures, there is no truly rational necessity for them to be moral. The Kantian principle of universalizability, on which so much moral theory in the West depends, is not really sound. According to that principle, one ought to treat the ends of others as on a par, rationally speaking, with one's own insofar as one shares with others morally relevant properties, such as the capacity to think or suffer. Reliance on this principle has lain behind the attempt, in much environmental ethics, to extend sentience to wider and wider circles of beings, on the assumption that mind, even in its barest sense, is the ground of all morally relevant properties. But even allowing this to be true, it does not follow that one is, as a discrete individual, bound by reason alone to treat the ends of others as on a par with one's own, since as a fully separate being one stands in a unique relation to one's own ends: I and I alone am in a position to satisfy most of my own needs. It is I who have to take breaths and place food in my mouth, for example, in order to stay alive, and no one else can perform these actions for me. I am, in other words, in a very special, immediate and urgent relation to my own interests, and it is not at all rational to suggest that the interests of others are, *for me*, on a par with my own. Morality is the *deus ex machina* used to try to repair the social and ecological unravelling that occurs when the world is understood, dissectively, in terms of discrete parts, units or individuals. The bedrock truth about morality as conceptualized within dissective frameworks however is that it is *not* binding.

The failure of dissective panpsychism to solve the problem of environmental ethics might then suggest that it is not dualism per se that is the ultimate root of our estrangement from reality, but the dissective or analysis-based explanatory presupposition of the Western tradition, and most particularly of science. Is it the assumption that in order to understand reality we must discover its constituents, the ultimate bits it is made of – whether these be construed as molecules, atoms or the ever more proliferating and ethereal units of elementary particle physics – that has set knowledge in the scientific era on the wrong track?

Simply trading our old view of the universe as a manifold of brute and blind particles for a view that adds to those particles a negligible glimmer of awareness then seems not significantly to alter either our metaphysical or moral orientation to reality. We might need rather to upend the traditional explanatory schema of science altogether, and start with a different question, not 'what is the universe built of?' but 'what is the nature of reality *as a whole?*'. Considering reality in this way, as in the first instance a seamless whole, we might then go on to ask, how does this whole unfold? What ensures its evident ongoing coherence *as* a whole? Is there a pattern, a dynamic of patterning, that inevitably generates this cohering? Depending on our answers to these questions, our own normative role as humans in this ongoing pattern of cohering may in due course become discernible. There might, in other words, prove to be a normative core to reality that would pre-empt our forlorn Western question, why be moral?

Questions such as those I have just listed are completely different from those that formed the launching pad for classical science. They require that we shift our metaphysical focus from the micro-level to the cosmological level, from the assumption that 'units' are the basis of explanation to an interest in the nature of the whole as a whole, with only a secondary interest in its 'parts'. This secondary interest is informed by an understanding that we cannot in any case discover the nature of the 'parts' before we discover the nature of the whole, since it is the nature of the latter that entails that of the former.

Why did classical scientists begin with the dissective assumption? Why did they take as their guiding question, what are the building blocks of reality? Why did this question seem to them – as it still does to most of us in the West today – the key to understanding reality? I shall return to this question in Lecture 4, where I shall suggest that the informal questions that guide formal inquiry are shaped unconsciously by the basic ways we inhabit our world and make our living in it – our *praxis*. If our praxis is building, as it is in settled agrarian and post-agrarian societies, then in asking about the nature of the world, we shall unconsciously be looking for its building blocks. As builders we take our environment apart and reassemble it to conform more closely to our own design. Pre-agrarian peoples, by contrast, acquiesce in the wholeness and completeness of their world. Reality is for them a seamless and sovereign system of affordances that can, if they play their proper role and align themselves to its needs, sustain them in perpetuity. Their question is thus not, what are the building blocks of this world – a question that would be pointless from their perspective – but, what is this proper role?

Let us then restart our inquiry from a holistic rather than a dissective perspective, and see whether this will show us reality and our relation to it in a fresh light, a light that can guide us towards closer alignment with it.

Lecture 2

IS OVERCOMING DUALISM ENOUGH? OR IS A HOLISTIC PERSPECTIVE ALSO REQUIRED?

What Might a Holistic Account of Reality Look Like?

Let us return then to the issue of worldview – of what is wrong with the Western worldview – again in light of our new hypothesis that the universe is not so much built up out of basic constituents – as classical physics supposed – but is primordially an *indivisible whole.* Let us see where this new metaphysical presupposition leads us in terms of understanding our place in the world.

When we contemplate the universe not as a contingent composite of components but as a seamless whole we may be tempted to ask, why is this universe, which stretches away from us in every direction in such breath-taking inter-galactic splendour, a *uni*verse, a unity: why does it cohere in the way that it apparently does? In asking this question we are however implicitly reverting to our default assumption that reality is compound, that it consists, as the eighteenth-century philosopher David Hume put it, of logically 'distinct existences', where it is this assumption that raises the question, why do these distinct existences hang together. If we set aside this assumption and assume instead that reality is not composed of distinct existences that are somehow held together by the (always contingent) laws of physics but that it is already a single indivisible unity, then different aspects of the universe may come to the fore as salient.

What we are likely to be struck by, when looking through this lens of unity, is not so much the various bodies that present – the stars, planets, rocks, grains of sand, cells, and so forth – as what lies between these bodies. In other words, we are likely to be struck by the fact that this universe is *spatial,* that all observable bodies are held, so to speak, in space, and that space itself is an indivisible continuum. Matter, by contrast, seems plainly divisible: we can cut it, and cut it again, all the way down to the level of subatomic particles. But we cannot cut space. We can differentiate different regions of space by reference to the bodies that appear to occupy them, but we cannot separate one 'part' of space from another, since this is an operation which itself could only take place in space.[1]

When space itself is viewed as the primary datum in this way, then distinct instances of matter can be reconciled with holism by being construed as local and transient deformations of space. Space can be viewed as an intrinsically dynamic terrain of wavelike motion – of ripple, current, eddy, whirlpool and flow. Such motion is wavelike since wavelikeness is the form that motion logically takes in a field that offers no resistance: it propagates at uniform speed in every direction. These wavelike disturbances in the fabric of space itself, and the patterns that form when they intersect, manifest to observers as physical forces of various kinds and, in their more stable configurations, as material phenomena. Such a geometrodynamics or 'space view of matter' is the vision that animated Einstein's holistically inclined General Theory of Relativity though it was a vision that could never be fulfilled in the highly dissective framework of physics within which Einstein was obliged to work (Mathews 1991).

When it is the spatial aspect of the universe that is seen as most salient, rather than its isolated instances of materiality, the first question that arises is not, what is the nature of matter, but rather, what is the nature of space? How are we to understand this vast, unbounded, unbroken, field-like continuum? Since it does not make sense to answer this question in our default manner, by explaining how space is built, we have to seek understanding of its nature in another way.

One way of accounting for the unboundedness and unbrokenness of space, its sheer fieldlikeness, is by supposing that an inner dimension – a dimension of subjectivity or mind – is integral to it. If space is in this way not merely a physical but a psychophysical manifold, with an inner as well as an outer aspect, and all instances of matter are merely disturbances within this psychophysical manifold, then the evident indivisibility and unboundedness of the universe, its necessary self-coherence into a unity, a *uni*verse, is explained. It is explained by virtue of the intrinsic nature of such a mental or subjectival inner dimension. For the felt quality of mind or subjectivity is intrinsically field-like, holistic, internally interpermeating, indivisible, unbounded. Subjectivity cannot be experienced as atomistic, as an aggregate of discrete

---

1 At the frontiers of particle physics, granular accounts of space are now postulated. This is not surprising given the highly dissective – particulate – paradigm within which the whole of physics is conceptualized. It does not however obviate the clear logical difference between space and matter in this connection – the fact that space cannot be physically partitioned in the way that matter can since the operation of parting one thing from another can only take place in space itself.

units of experience or even as a continuum of point-like experiences. If sub-jectivity, or mentality more generally, is as primal as physicality in the overall scheme of things, then physical existence must reflect the indivisible nature of mind. Physicality must exhibit the same field-like structure as mind (Mathews 2003, 2011).

Another question that quickly follows on the heels of the first as we pursue this line of inquiry is, why is mind itself field-like and indivisible? A possible answer is that mentality is a function of *meaning*. In speaking of meaning I am not referring simply to the meanings of words or other communicative gestures but to the deeper sense of meaningfulness that is core to all things with an interest in their own existence. For things, or rather beings, that are shaped by such an investment in their own existence, everything that is going on around them potentially matters to them. Different goings-on matter to them in different ways. Some are conducive to their continued existence; oth-ers threaten that existence; many do neither but, in combination with further factors, may come to do so. Beings with an interest in their own existence thus register – cognize – different aspects of their environment differentially in accordance with these shifting possibilities of salience, and this is the beginning of meaning and the root of cognition. Meaning, in other words, enters the world as a dimension of self-mattering. But meaning is by its nature demonstrably indivisible – different meanings pervade, inter-permeate and inflect one another, morphing according to context. (Think of the layering of meaning that renders good poetry resistant to analysis.) Mind, as the medium of meaningfulness, must share this field-like quality of indivisibility (Mathews 1991, 2007).

If mind is tied in this way to meaning, and meaning is in turn tied to the sense of meaningfulness that is the province of beings with an intrin-sic investment in their own existence, then our present line of questioning suggests that the universe considered under the aspect of its evident whole-ness, and hence as imbued with mind, must likewise be invested in its own existence.

The idea of a being with an intrinsic investment in its own existence is not as mysterious as it might at first appear. Looking around us, we can readily observe in our own environment beings with such an investment in their own existence and hence with a constitutive sense of self-mattering and self-meaning. Here on Earth, we are indeed surrounded by such beings: they include organisms as well, arguably, as higher order systems such as ecosystems and perhaps Earth itself. Living systems – systems so configured that they actively seek to maintain themselves in existence by their own self-referring efforts – abound, and we ourselves are of course numbered amongst them.

It might be inferred then, in a prima facie way, that the universe as a whole is a system or being of this kind: it is systemically organized to maintain itself in existence by its own self-referring efforts. The seventeenth-century philosopher, Baruch Spinoza, had a term for such a will to self-existence: *conatus* or conativity. A conative being or system has a constitutive interest in self-realization – self-actualization, self-maintenance and self-increase. I call such conative beings or systems, *selves*.

If mind, as a function of meaning and ultimately of self-mattering, is the province of selves, and the universe as a whole has an inner, mental dimension, as its presumed seamless wholeness suggests, then the universe as a whole must qualify as a self – a very special, *sui generis* kind of self, or Self, indeed, but a self nonetheless – self-actualizing, self-preserving and self-expanding.

The entire manifest or empirical world, in both its minutest detail and its vastest scope, would from this point of view figure as the 'outward' appearance of an inner field of conative experience, the experience of a cosmological Self. Since this inner field is mental and hence necessarily indivisible and self-cohering, the outer universe will also partake of such coherence and indivisibility, thus accounting for the holism that our inquiry has presupposed.

An alert reader might wonder how the universe as a whole might be viewed 'from the outside', since nothing, *ex hypothesi*, exists outside it? One might reply that although this universe coheres as a unity, it also evidently undergoes self-differentiation: it is not merely a field of 'empty' space but is rather subject to disturbance in endless dynamic or motive combinations and permutations. Such internal self-differentiation on the part of a conative system must furthermore be understood as an aspect of its self-realization and self-increase. Its field-like fabric ripples and folds locally to form a dynamic manifold of ever-changing, finite configurations, like the waves, whirlpools and eddies on the surface of the ocean. To borrow another term from Spinoza, we might call these transient, local configurations in the fabric of reality, 'modes' of the cosmic unity since they are not discrete entities in their own right but disturbances in the cosmic fabric.

Amongst these modes or differentia we find some – a select subset – that have undergone sufficient (though always relative) individuation to count as self-realizing configurations in their own right, thereby distinguishing themselves, from within their own perspective, from the surrounding field. Such special modes consist, in other words, in local patterns in the underlying psychophysical field which are so configured as to perpetuate themselves, by their own efforts, against environmental inroads into their integrity, in the manner of relatively stable or standing waves in a fluid. Modes of this type qualify as (relative) selves. It is from the relatively self-contained per-spective of such selves, situated within the wider field but actively differen-tiating themselves from it, that reality may be said to present an 'outward' appearance.

This intuitive line of argument then, that started not with the question of the building blocks of reality but rather with the fact of its demonstrable self-coherence, has brought us back to panpsychism, but to a cosmological version thereof that I call *living cosmos panpsychism* (Mathews 2017a). According to my account of living cosmos panpsychism – which owes a lot to Spinoza – the empirical world, the world of òur senses, is the outward appearance of an inner, felt field of subjectivity, where subjectivity is understood as the sense of self-presence that is a pre-condition for experience. Reality is, from this point of view, both a unity and a manifold of finite modes or differentia, a One and a Many. Viewed from within, it is a felt global field of subjectivity, with a conativity of its own – a will to realize itself and increase its own existence. From the viewpoint of its finite modes, however, or those of them that are so configured as to act as observers, it is the external manifold of space-in-time that we apprehend via our senses (Mathews 2003).[2]

When finite selves are understood as modes of a cosmos – a larger Self – that is structured in accordance with its own conative ends, we might surmise with some confidence that those selves must themselves be intended, in some sense, to contribute in their own small, but perhaps special, ways to those larger ends: the purpose of their existence within this larger scheme must ultimately be to further the self-realization and self-increase of the cosmos.

How to Align with a Living Cosmos?

How might finite selves contribute to the unfolding of cosmo-conativity? How in particular might we as *human* selves contribute to this unfolding? Two ways seem to emanate from the living cosmos perspective: firstly, we need to dis-cover and reflectively align ourselves with what might be called *Law*; and secondly, we are called to enter into *communication* with this living cosmos. Let me explain.

---

2 Cosmological versions of panpsychism are currently surfacing as a theoretical option in the philosophy of mind (Goff 2019; Shani 2015; Nagasawa and Wager 2016), but such an outlook has much deeper roots in the history of Western thought. (Skrbina 2005) In that latter history such theories originated not specifically as a response to the riddle of consciousness but as a speculative response to the primordial question of metaphysics: what is the ultimate nature of reality. It is on these older and more primordial origins that my own account draws for its inspiration. (Mathews 1991)

Law

As a locus of conativity the living cosmos is itself already organized around an axis of value: its self-structuring activity implies, while at the same time constituting, a primal *good*, namely its own self-perpetuation and self-increase. This is the form in which value per se originates. As modes of the conative fabric of this cosmos, we finite selves also fall under that value: we must try to discover how best to serve the primal good, how best to contribute to the ongoing actualization and increase of this self-cohering cosmos. There is in this sense an 'ought' at the core of the living cosmos of which we, as finite selves, need to be mindful. This 'ought' or immanent normativity might be described as *Law* (Mathews 2019a, 2021). A clue to the nature of Law, to the innate pattern of unfolding that sustains a living cosmos, may arguably be found, once again, in living systems. For this is a *synergic* pattern, one of mutually accommodating conativities, or, as I have termed it, a pattern characterized by the twin principles of (i) conativity, and (ii) accommodation and least resistance (Mathews 2011a, 2019a). In the biosphere, the behaviour of most species broadly follows these twin principles since this is a strategy that, being energy-conserving, logically results from natural selection.

Let us consider these twin principles in a little more detail. In the living world, species known as ecosystem engineers provide perhaps the best example of how conativity, shaped by the requirement of accommodation and least resistance, assures the ongoing integrity and stability of larger ecological wholes. Since the term 'engineer' has mechanical connotations inconsistent with a conative view of ecosystems, let us replace it with the term 'landscaper'. A classic instance of an ecological landscaper is the beaver. Seeking shelter, safe from torrents and predators, beavers dam waterways to create still ponds in which stick lodges may be conveniently constructed. Beaver dams modify and redirect stream flows, in the process hydrating the landscape, mitigating floods, filtering runoff and creating wetlands that provide habitat for myriads of other plant and animal species. These biodiverse and healthy wetlands in turn afford necessary conditions for healthy waterways and hence for healthy beavers (Goldfarb 2018).

Here in Australia, ecological landscapers include the 'little diggers', an array of small marsupials and monotremes, such as bandicoots, bilbies, bettongs and echidnas, as well as the iconic lyrebird (Fleming 2013; Maisey 2021). These animals dig for truffles in the case of bettongs; soil invertebrates, tubers and seeds in the case of bandicoots and bilbies; ants, in the case of echidnas; and a variety of soil invertebrates and small vertebrates in the case of lyrebirds. In the process of digging, they turn over and thereby aerate woodland soils, and they do so on a grand scale: a single lyrebird is estimated to move on average 155 tonnes of soil and leaf litter per hectare per year, this being equivalent to 11 standard dump truck loads. Aeration boosts microbial activity and increases litter decomposition rates while improving water retention and filtration and preventing soil erosion. Higher decomposition rates reduce the volume of leaf litter, thereby lowering fuel load in woodlands, rendering them more resistant to extreme fires. The particular patterns of soil disturbance that result from digging also serve to cycle nutrients and excavate hollows for seed germination.[3]

In a variety of ways, then, such diggers, merely acting in accordance with their own inclinations, help to assure the future of the woodlands and hence the future of the resources on which they themselves depend. The healthy woodland, for its part, freely gives what these animals desire, thereby sparing them the effort of providing it for themselves. When each party adapts its conativity to that of its ecological neighbours in this way, desiring only and precisely what its neighbours need it to desire, all sustain themselves in energy-conserving ways, thereby enhancing their respective chances of survival. The relation of the ecological landscaper to its environment is a classic instance of synergy, if we understand synergy as a 'process whereby two parties join their conativities to create a new end which subsumes, but at the same time enlarges, the respective conativities of each party' (Mathews 2011a, 373).

Conflict, competition and predation do of course occur in nature. Often the synergic pattern is evident only at the population level rather than at the level of individuals. Predation, for example, is essential to prevent populations of herbivores from over-grazing the grasslands on which they depend, though the relation between predator and prey as individuals can hardly in itself be construed as synergic. In cases in which parties cannot achieve synergy at all, whether at the individual or population level, conflict may occur. But since such conflict will always entail an energy cost for the individuals or populations in question, modes of conflict themselves will tend to be shaped by the principle of least resistance: antagonists who favour efficacious but less energy-intensive modes of combat will be favoured by the logic of natural selection. (Martial arts follow this model: practitioners learn to conserve their own energy by turning the force used by opponents back onto those opponents.) At the end of the day, the imperative to desire what others

---

3 See   https://www.latrobe.edu.au/news/articles/2020/release/lyrebirds-natures-eco-system-engineers, accessed 3 Jan 2022.

need one to desire will be what ensures that every living thing, in effortlessly following its own inclination, at the same time perpetuates the larger system that satisfies it.

Within the specificity of different environmental circumstances, then, such adaptivity to the ends of others helps to shape the morphology and functionality of each organism. Working together, the two principles result in complex synergies of mutual accommodation: each organism seeks its own existence in ways that help to perpetuate the existence of the organisms surrounding it. In aggregate, such mutually adaptive organisms make up larger, self-perpetuating systems. This is not to say that new mutations producing life forms that fail to follow the principle of accommodation may not arise, but only that when they do, they will in due course be selected out of existence. At the end of the day, the principle of accommodating others by adapting one's own desires to theirs is what assures the ongoing regeneration of life.

Although this logic of synergy applies to ourselves just as it does to other forms of life, our high degree of reflexive awareness confers on us an unusual degree of freedom with respect to ends: our ends are subject to variable cultural influences and may not follow instinctual patterns laid down through evolutionary processes. Such culturally mediated ends may, in consequence, depart from the principle of synergy and clash or conflict with the ends of others. We may be ready to trade off the effort expended in such conflict against the gratification we anticipate from doing as we please. As beings highly endowed with reflexive awareness, then, we can choose to depart from Law and act instead in an 'impose and control' mode. We have gotten away with doing this without depleting ourselves only because we have co-opted sources of energy external to ourselves, such as those afforded by domesticated animals, slaves and, in more recent times, fossil fuels. However, self-depletion was only one of the selective consequences of the impose-and-control mode; the other was the depletion of the environment that sustains the imposer. The imposer eventually selects itself out of existence by thwarting the conativities of the systems that support it.

Although there is a logic to synergy then, it must be understood as a *normative* principle rather than in strictly deterministic terms. That is why I call it Law with a capital 'L': the Law of the living cosmos. Though not a law in the sense of the causal regularities codified by physics, let alone in the sense of a mere juridical convention as per the legal systems of the West, it is core to the riddle of existence per se. For it is a law of *energy*, the conative energy that seeks existence in the first place. Accommodation and least resistance represent the logic that preserves and increases the conative field, the field of being. This is why I think it is not too much to say that Law in this sense is an 'ought' at the very root of the cosmic 'is'.

Let us note too that from the perspective of Law there is no substantive division between humans and the rest of nature. Indeed, 'nature' is understood from this perspective not substantively, in terms of trees and rocks and everything else that is not human, but processually, as how things unfold when everything is following the pattern of synergy, the twin principles of conativity and accommodation/least resistance. Highly reflexive beings such as ourselves, subject to variable cultural influences, can, as we have remarked, choose whether or not to conform to Law. When our desires depart from Law, we become outsiders, no longer part of nature. When they conform to Law, however, we become part of nature again, regardless of whether we find ourselves mid-metropolis or in the wildest and most far-flung of places.

Communicativity

Why does the living cosmos differentiate itself in such a way that finite selves, under the guidance of Law, are enabled to inscribe themselves into its fabric? Is there a special part that selves can play in the self-realization of the cosmos? One possibility is that the existence of such selves offers communicative opportunities to the cosmos itself – opportunities for exchanges of meaning and perspective with those of its self-realizing modes that are capable of such engagement. This in turn may represent an opportunity for cosmic self-increase in the sense that self-increase may be understood as proceeding not merely on an extensional plane, as expansion or complexification in space, but on an inner or experiential plane, as a deepening of self-meaning. Such deepening can surely only be achieved through communicative exchanges of perspective with others. Our own case is illustrative in this connection: we know that the consciousness of a human self, deprived of opportunities for communicative engagement with other humans, would be irremediably stunted. Indeed, if meaning springs from the differential values that a conative being, bent on preserving and increasing its own existence, ascribes to the various aspects of its environment as it negotiates its precarious way through the world, then what meaning could there be for a cosmic Self for whom no such environment exists? If the cosmos configures finite selves within its own fabric through processes of self-differentiation, however, then those relative selves become loci of meaning, in communication with whom the cosmos self-actualizes as a subjectival field. In this sense, enabling relative selves to constellate within its fabric, and furthermore engaging them in communicative exchange, may be a necessary and primary frontier for the inner – and hence also outer – actualization of the cosmos.

But how could such communicative engagement occur? In this context we might speak of the possibility of a *poetic* order – an order of poetic revelation – unfolding alongside the more familiar *causal* order of events. By 'poetic order' I mean an order of meaningful configurations of circumstances that constellate as a result of *invocation* on our part: when we as finite selves invoke the world, in terms drawn from our own particular narrative or poetic frames of reference, the world may choose to respond by arranging itself to match those terms. The terms in question will be unavoidably *poetic*, in the sense of metaphorical, since the only 'language' available to the world is a language of *things*. The world cannot literally address us in speech, but it can synchronistically arrange concrete particulars in meaningful configurations in the same way that poetry and dreams use imagery to create and convey meaning. Instances of such poetic engagement between self and world might be described as instances of *ontopoetics* (Mathews 2017a). Though this poetic order will exceed the causal order, inasmuch as it partakes of intentionality – it carries meaning in response to specific instances of address – it will not contradict the causal order; it is not an order of miracles.

The world's religions and folk traditions provide a treasury of instances of ontopoetics and of invocational rituals and ceremonies that may activate the cosmos under its communicative aspect. The Old Testament is overflowing with such instances – from the burning bush encountered by Moses to the Israelites' pillar of fire by night and cloud by day to the rainbow that appeared to Noah when the great flood subsided. Such 'signs' may be seen as ontopoetic responses to the Judaic narratives that framed particular acts or states of invocation – particular ceremonies – amongst the ancient Jewish people. Indeed, rainbows seem to have figured as an ontopoetic trope in many traditions, from the rainbow bodies of enlightened lamas in Tibet to Rainbow Serpent manifestations in Indigenous Australia to rainbows as bridging worlds in Norse and Japanese mythology.

But the ontopoetic lexicon that frames a given act or state of invocation need not be drawn only from the narratives of established religions or folk traditions. Individuals may discover, in the course of a lifetime, a story or numinous image that seems to answer to their own particular truth – a story or image that can serve for them as a guiding symbol or myth. It might offer itself from some ancient source or arrive freshly minted by way of a Big Dream visited upon the individual himself or herself. He or she might then adopt this story or symbol as a poetic frame for ceremony – for an intentional act of invocation – where such an act might take various forms, including that of journey or pilgrimage. Journeys or pilgrimages do indeed seem to have particular ontopoetic force. But larger gatherings with ritual intent, conducted in landscape, can be efficacious too. As can more formal inquiries in academic contexts dedicated to exploring possibilities of dialogical exchange with reality (Kurio and Reason 2021; Poelina and Wooltorton 2020, 2021). Whether the ontopoetic frame for invocation features gods or God, ancestors or totems, mountains or landscapes, geometric motifs, spirits or Mystery or private dreams, the ontopoetic response will emanate, if it emanates at all, from the living cosmos under its inner aspect, the measureless depths of a subjectivity that is never exhausted by singular manifestation.

We have arrived then at a metaphysical or cosmological template that effectively upends the Newtonian template that has underpinned the instrumentalism that has driven the rise of modern industrial civilization. It is clear just how far we must depart from that Newtonian template in order truly to escape the mind-set of instrumentalism. It is not enough simply to tackle *dualism*, by 'restoring' mind to animals, plants, ecosystems, or even to objects like rocks or grains of sand or any or all of the various micro-particles. This move retains the root presupposition that to say what reality *is*, and hence to figure out how we should comport ourselves in relation to it, is to say what its *constituents* are – how it is built from the ground up. But no such ontology of 'distinct existences' can, as we have seen, show us how we, as reflexive beings with a conativity of our own no longer fully determined by biological inheritance, *ought* to act. Only when reality is apprehended under its holistic aspect can we recognize that the conative core of the cosmos is in fact also the core of our own conativity; as modes of this greater cosmo-conativity, we ourselves fall under an overarching imperative, an Ought that permeates the very fabric of existence.

Aboriginal Law and Living Cosmos Panpsychism

In pre-agrarian societies, in which peoples lived in deep synergy with local ecosystems rather than overriding them with designs of their own, such a normative pattern in the fabric of reality was self-evident and often also described as Law. Law was explicitly acknowledged – and is still acknowledged today by many peoples who have managed to retain continuity with Indigenous ways of life – as immanent in the fabric of Creation.

We shall return to a discussion of Law in Lecture 3, with particular reference to the parallel notion of *Dao*, which arguably still nourishes the deepest roots of Chinese civilization. For the moment, however, let us compare Law, in a preliminary way, to its counterpart in contemporary pre-agrarian societies. Aboriginal Australia offers a wealth of evidence in this connection. According to Deborah Bird Rose in her classic ethnography, *Dingo Makes Us Human*, based on research with the people of Yarralin in Northern Territory, Law may be characterized in terms of four norms: *balance, symmetry, autonomy*

and *response*. *Balance* must be achieved between competing interests or oppos-
ing forces, all of which must be treated as *symmetric* in the sense of equal in
respect of moral considerability, with none being regarded as in any sense less
than or properly subservient to others. Each, in other words, must be treated
as 'boss for itself', as an entity endowed with *autonomous* agency. All such agencies are required to acknowledge and adapt to the wider fields of agency that
surround them by way of continuous two-way, or *responsive*, communication.
When these four norms – which effectively revolve around the axis of balance
– are observed, Rose notes, *sustaining relationships* are preserved – between
people and people, people and other species, species and species, species
and country, country and country. The cosmos, as governed by Law in this
Aboriginal sense, is a normative order, inasmuch as every being, whether
human or non-human, has its own will (conativity), and can choose whether
or not to play its part in keeping the system of relationships knitted up. To
disregard Law is to allow the cosmos to unravel (Rose 1992).

Yarralin Law is, moreover, according to Rose, encoded not merely in
empirical relationships and correlations in the local landscape but in *stories*,
stories that emanate from every aspect and element of that landscape. This
points to a meaning dimension that lies hidden within the manifest world: the
outer landscape expresses an inner communion amongst entities, from the
smallest to the largest scale. Although there are multiple words for this inner
dimension in Aboriginal languages, each with its own unique set of connotations, it is generally rendered in English as *Dreaming*; stories that reveal those
inner meanings to humans are known as Dreamings. As an interviewee of
Rose, Mussolini Harvey from the Gulf of Carpentaria in northern Australia,
explains:

> The Dreamings made our Law … .This Law is the way we live, our
> rules. This Law is our ceremonies, our songs, our stories; all of these
> things came from the Dreaming. … our Law is not like European
> [l]aw which is always changing – new government, new laws; but our
> Law cannot change, we did not make it. The Law was made by the
> Dreamings many, many years ago and given to our ancestors and they
> gave it to us. … The Dreamings are our ancestors, no matter if they are
> fish, birds, men, women, animals, wind or rain. It was these Dreamings
> that made our Law. All things in our country have Law, they have cer-
> emony and song … (Harvey quoted in Rose 1996, 26)

Philosopher and Kombumerri Elder, Mary Graham, offers an account of
Aboriginal Law that resonates strongly with Rose's account of Yarralin Law.
While emphasizing the complexity and diversity of articulations of Law

across the continent, she emphasizes two commonalities. Firstly, the Law is in the land: it is not a mere human construct. Secondly, it is underpinned by a relational ethos understood in terms of four principles: custodialism, locality, autonomy and balance. Together, these principles promote reciprocity, not hierarchy, amongst people themselves and between people and their local ecologies. Law thus, according to Graham's account, emanates from the inherently relational structure of reality: humans, she writes, are not alone. 'They are *connected and made* by way of relationships with a wide range of beings.' Aboriginal people grasp this essential relationality because they perceive 'a psychic level of natural behaviour, the behaviour of natural entities' (Graham 2019, 6).

Aboriginal notions of Law and Dreaming then seem resonant with a panpsychist view that posits an inner dimension of meaning, normativity and communicativity as integral to the self-constituting, self-cohering unfolding of a living cosmos.

So What Is Civilization?

When Europeans first colonized Australia over two hundred years ago, they regarded Aboriginal peoples as 'savage', and, shamefully, this view has lingered throughout the colonial history of Australia. Aboriginal thought has rarely been included in modern philosophical discourse. Yet Aboriginal culture has the longest continuous history of any human society, ever. At least 50,000 years, and the estimates of its duration are continually being revised upwards. A culture that can endure for so long, through such enormous climatic and geological vicissitudes, surely has incomparable adaptivity. Aboriginal societies, at the time of European contact, had one of the simplest material technologies of any known society. They had little in the way of clothing, buildings or transport systems. Their material tools, though ingenious, were minimal – digging sticks, boomerangs, bark canoes and bowls, fish traps, grinding stones, didgeridoos. But this was deceptive: they had other 'technologies' that were invisible to European eyes because they did not consist of artefacts. These included 'technologies' such as the intentional and highly nuanced use of fire and water as well regenerative techniques for hand-harvesting staple species.

In the case of fire, for instance, Aboriginal people were skilled at lightly and highly selectively burning the landscape, using different rotations for different ecosystems and even for different individual plants, applying fire in ways that were responsive to seasonal, geographic and any number of other relevant conditions. These fire regimes rendered the country reliably productive for Aboriginal people's needs, modifying ecosystems without degrading them.

Burning was particularly sensitive to the pattern of water flows in the country, to the need to maintain deep layers of spongy, water-retentive organic top-soil to ensure the ongoing hydration of the landscape (Gammage 2011; Steffensen 2020). The disastrous mismanagement of fire, water and soil in Australia since colonization has resulted in increased dehydration and combustibility as well as ecological degradation on a continental scale. Consistently with their use and understanding of both fire and water, Aboriginal people also devised simple but judicious techniques of digging and selective harvesting of staple but still wild plant species to increase populations of those species in ways that benefited not only people but the ecosystem at large (Pascoe 2014). In this sense they worked with the natural grain of things, tailoring their own conativity to the needs of their fellow species.

It was thus knowledge rather than an elaborate material culture that enabled Aboriginal peoples to flourish in Australia on a geological time scale; they relied on deep understanding of and communicative engagement with natural processes to guide those processes in ways that served the interests of all aspects of the ecosocial system. The material simplicity of such a culture, so disparaged by Europeans, was precisely the measure of its fitness: people needed nothing more than this knowledge in order to flourish. Being materially unencumbered, moreover, they were free to move easily during periods of climate disturbance or other forms of natural disruption. There was no heavy material superstructure or 'civilization' to come crashing down, as modern civilization is perhaps likely to do in the near, climate-deranged future.

Meanwhile, Aboriginal societies also exhibited an exemplary humanity, to which poverty, political subjugation, social marginalization, criminality and large-scale warfare, the hallmarks of so-called civilization, were alien. They inhabited a kinship-oriented culture in which everyone and everything – seen and unseen – had its inalienable and honourable place in a Lawful cosmos. This approach in fact left Aboriginal people more secure and better nourished than most peoples throughout the history of civilizations. Writing in 1770, Captain Cook himself, the navigator and explorer who laid claim to the Australian continent on behalf of the British, described Aborigines as the 'happiest people upon the face of the earth' (Lucashenko 2013).

Europeans equated civilization not with happiness, humaneness, kinship with Earth and ecological prosperity but with material culture – with the kind of clutter of commodities generally derived from wealth amassed via often cruel regimes of inequality, exploitation and inhumanity. Blinded by this assumption, Europeans remained insensible – until recently – to the sophistication of Aboriginal culture. The fact of this sophistication is now finally dawning on non-Indigenous Australia, and there is consequently greater readiness to use Aboriginal thinking as a lens through which to critique our contemporary context (Yunkaporta 2020). In light of this it seems time to review the concept of civilization itself.

The notion of city is core to that of civilization: the word 'civilization' derives from the Latin *civitas*, meaning city. Cities are associated with sedentary, economically and socially stratified, usually literate, administratively centralized, but above all *agrarian*-based societies of the kind that originated in the Neolithic and predominate in the world today. Such societies tend to be characterized by monumental architecture, sophisticated weaponry and artisanry made possible by complex systems of division of labour and specialization of economic roles, systems that have in due course emanated in the thoroughgoing industrialism of modern civilization. Civilization in this root descriptive sense tends, in other words, to be defined in contrast to hunter-gatherer societies and other subsistence-based forms of society. But the term, 'civilization', is also used prescriptively, as denoting a more advanced stage of social development than may be found in smaller-scale, subsistence societies. It is this coupling of the descriptive and prescriptive that needs to be challenged in our revision of the concept. The Aboriginal example demonstrates that a society may be economically and socially unstratified, administratively decentralized, based on forms of land care and custody that do not conform to traditional definitions of agriculture, and guided by mnemonically based rather than literacy-based knowledge-systems, and yet arguably count as more 'advanced' than the societies traditionally lauded as paradigm instances of civilization. Indeed, if we hold to the prescriptive rather than descriptive sense of the term, the Aboriginal example suggests a radical reversal of customary conceptions of civilization: societies which can sustain the health, longevity, security, dignity and *joie de vivre* of their people by way of a culture rooted in deep understanding of the indwelling meaning of the cosmos rather than in manufacture may claim to be more advanced, and in this sense more civilized, than societies that merely boast high levels of material culture.

Lecture 3

BUT IS HOLISTIC THEORY EVEN POSSIBLE? WHAT DOES IT MEAN TO KNOW THE WORLD HOLISTICALLY?

Why Has the Dissective Tendency Been So Persistent in the West?

In Lecture 2, I proposed living cosmos panpsychism as a holistic alternative to the dissective outlook of modern science with its dissociating implications for our relationship with nature. But in fact, holistic versions of panpsychism have figured significantly in the Western tradition; Spinoza is a prominent case in point. Yet such theories have always remained outriders to the main intellectual traditions, both in philosophy itself and in the cultural mainstream. In the modern period – by which I mean from the time of the Scientific Revolution in the seventeenth century – the West has, as we have seen, adhered very strongly to its dissective presupposition, a presupposition that rules out the possibility of intrinsic normativity, or Law, in nature. In consequence, our attitude of dominate-and-control with respect to the natural world has only continued to gain strength.

So perhaps merely coming up with a *theory* that conforms to holism and thereby seeks to supersede our old dissective or atomizing habits of thinking will not enable us to check this stubborn tendency. It might in addition be necessary to scrutinize *why* these dissective or atomizing habits of thought have become so entrenched. Is there something not just in *what* we think but about the *way* we think that disposes us to see the world in these divide-and-rule terms?

I shall suggest that there is and that to understand this disposition we need to dig down beneath the explicit content of theories and examine the underlying thought processes that are involved in the mental production of theory itself. We need, in other words, to examine the *phenomenology* of theorizing – to ask ourselves what it feel like, subjectively, when we are theorizing. When the phenomenology of theorizing is examined in this way, we shall discover that the theoretical mode of cognition, which had its origins in the philosophy of ancient Greece, in fact enacts an inner disjunction between subject and object that then endlessly plays itself out as a divisive tendency in the theories it spawns, a tendency that ultimately cancels out the possibility of a holistic worldview.

Theoria and strategia

It was a brilliant article by the French philosopher and sinologist Francois Jullien that first alerted me to the fact that the cognitive process of theorizing might itself be the problem in this connection: the source of our modern mistake might be traceable not merely to our metaphysics, which is to say, our theories about the nature of reality, but to our epistemology, our way of knowing or thinking about the world.

As an environmental philosopher, I had, as detailed in the previous lecture, been part of the project of developing a theoretical – ultimately panpsychist – alternative to the atomist paradigm we have inherited from classical science. As philosophers, we saw ourselves as engaged in a contest of truths – a contest in which we sought to replace the ostensible truths of the prevailing, basically atomist worldview with what we considered to be the genuine truths of a more relational, ecological worldview. But Jullien's article, 'Did philosophers have to become fixated on truth?' (Jullien 2002), signalled the possible contingency of truth itself as the goal of cognition. And it was the meta-level contrast Jullien drew between the figure of the ancient Greek philosopher and that of the Chinese sage that made this contingency of truth as a goal plain to me. Jullien observes that while the philosopher set out to *explain* the world, to provide an accurate and exhaustive representation of it, the sage sought *congruence* with the world – he set out to *adapt* or *accommodate* himself to it. The sage sought to identify the tendencies already at work in particular situations in order to align his own ends with them. His ends accordingly needed to be flexible – he could not afford for them to become fixed by ideology or conviction; for this reason, he remained pragmatically open to all points of view instead of insisting, as philosophers did, on a single representation (viz 'the truth'), exclusive of others. In describing the thinking of the sage in these terms, Jullien seemed to imply that such thinking remained embedded in agency rather than becoming, like the thinking of the Greeks, an end in itself. Clearly the philosopher and the sage were operating with very different, indeed contrasting, models of knowledge.

Taking this intriguing cue from Jullien, let us try to reconstruct the cognitive processes that occur when philosophers – ancient or modern – seek truth. (In venturing into this phenomenological terrain, here and in the rest of this lecture, I am extrapolating beyond the starting point that Jullien himself provides.) Consider the case of a thinker who, like the earliest Greek philoso-phers, is conducting a proto-metaphysical inquiry: he is investigating, at a purely intellectual level, the ultimate nature of reality. His method involves a particular mental or cognitive operation: he holds an inner, abstract mirror up to the world-as-revealed-through-the-senses and in that mirror he constructs a systematic account of the underlying principles or laws that explain why the world, or an aspect of it, presents the appearance that it does to the senses. If this abstract schema – his theory – is found to correspond, in some sense, to the world of appearances, then the theory is considered true (Mathews 2009). The truth about reality, or some aspect or portion of reality, is of course ideal, and for that reason permanent: the real world changes; things perish and pass away, but the truth about the world does not change; the truth about things is timeless. Theory thus enables the philosopher to capture the world, pin it down, through truth. Through discovering its truth he makes it his own; in a certain sense he co-opts it. For this reason, truth becomes the philosopher's goal and the 'grasping' of truth is deemed an end in itself.

Such a notion of truth as an end in itself arguably did not crystallize in other ancient societies to quite the same degree that it did amongst the Greeks. While there were lively cultures of public reason, rhetoric and debate around social and political concerns in many ancient societies, including China, thinking about the cosmos at large tended to remain inextricable from myth, religion and oracle (Graeber and Windrow 2021). In apprehending the cos-mos under mythopoetic aspects, people positioned themselves as agents or supplicants in relation to powerful supernatural forces and figures, seeking help or guidance. They did not position themselves as detached spectators in search of ideal schemas that could stand in for reality, as the Greeks did. Philosophy in this theoretical, Greek sense is accordingly sometimes regarded as establishing the distinctive tone, the root form of cognition, for Western civilization (Lent 2017).

Notice however that in apprehending the world in an ideal, theoretic mode we are interpreting it under a peculiarly disembodied aspect, reflec-tive of what-is but inert, unable to act upon the observer or be acted upon by them. While such idealization of the object of knowledge was not histori-cally accomplished all at once in Greece, and traces of the older supernatu-ral narratives lingered in the philosophizing of the earliest Greek thinkers, it did become dramatically explicit in Plato, in the shape of the Theory of Forms. The Forms were the abstract, eternal, perfect and unchanging images to which any actual, concrete, perishable world must conform. The goal of thought, according to Plato, was to access this abstract realm and apprehend reality under its timeless aspect. But in positing Forms, Plato was really no more than reifying the phenomenology of the act of theorizing. By projecting an idealized schema of the world onto a kind of abstract screen in an inner theatre, the mind constitutes theory. This mental process has left its trace in etymology: the word 'theory' (like 'theatre') is derived from the Greek *theoria*, a looking at, thing looked at; *theoros*, spectator; and *thea*, spectacle.[1]

In the process of theorizing, then, the human mind subtly removes itself from reality and becomes reality's spectator, an observer of the drama but also its author, invisible from within the constructed drama itself and in this sense invested with a status different from the elements of that drama, the elements of the re-presented reality. From this stance two momentous consequences follow.

1) The knower who could not be included in his own schema – his own ideal map or model of reality – was, I would suggest, the original *subject*, and the world as ideal projection, or re-presentation in the theatre of the subject's mind, the original *object*. In other words, it was via the subtle reification involved in *theoria*, the introjective act of reflective knowing, that the world first became an object for the human mind, inert and untouchable and completely devoid of real presence or agency of its own. In this separation of active, world-constructing subject from the merely acted-upon, constructed object, dualism finds expression not merely at a descriptive level but as a distinctive cognitive modality in its own right: dualism is enacted via the subject-object bifurcation that structures the process of theorizing. Qua knower, the subject is categorically different from the mere after-image of the world that it projects onto its mental screen, and as a result it inevitably feels the sense of apartness from, and aloofness to, the world that we witness in the history of Western thought. Insofar as the subject views the world through a theoretic lens, then, he or she is disposed not to recognize, in any deeply felt way, the independent subjectivity of abstractly re-presented others. The experience of theorizing will in this way psychologically block any attempt to ascribe independent subjectivity to the world at large. However rationally feasible our attempted theorizations of the subjectivity of others may be, they will contradict our own phenomenological experience as theorists. For this reason, panpsychist theories of any kind will, in the theory-based culture at large, lack traction.

2) The second – already intimated – consequence of this inner bifurcation into subject and object is even more far reaching in its implications for knowledge. No matter how encompassing the abstract map or model of reality that the knower constructs is intended to be, it can never, as something created by the subject, include the subject itself amongst its contents. In attempting to include itself in its own theory, the subject unavoidably objectifies itself,

---

1 See Online Etymological Dictionary, <https://www.etymonline.com/word/theory>.

thereby contradicting the very subjectivity involved in its act of producing theory. At a phenomenological level, then, theorizing logically precludes the possibility of holism; it always leaves a gap at the centre of reality that breaks up any possibility of wholeness.

The import of this latter point however is not merely phenomenological. If the theorizing subject cannot be included amongst the contents of its own abstract schema, then this implies that reality under its holistic aspect is actually untheorizable. The thinking subject is, after all, clearly *something*; it exists, it is active. But if this existence, this activity, cannot figure in any theoretical representation of the universe, then no such representation can claim to encompass the whole of reality. This is as true of the cosmological version of panpsychism outlined in Lecture 2 as it is of any other purportedly holistic theory.

If this is the case, we might wonder whether reality under its holistic aspect can be known at all? Perhaps it can, but only via a very different way of knowing. To see this, let us return for a moment to Jullien's Chinese sage. Where the Greek philosopher became mesmerized by abstract representation and the products of his own thought, retreating to a 'life of the mind', the Chinese sage, according to Jullien, remained immersed in the tangible here and now. His goal was not the abstract one of arriving at 'truth' but was rather to discover how life could be lived more effectively. His definitive discovery in this connection, according to Jullien, was that one lives most effectively by *accommodating* oneself to one's environment. In seeking to identify the tendencies or dispositions at work in particular situations, one must not so much theorize concerning them but actively, bodily, practically, orient oneself to them in pursuit of one's own conative ends.

Let us describe sages in this sense as *strategists*. (Again, neither strategy (*strategia*) nor theory (*theoria*) are terms used by Jullien – I am using his contrast between the Greek philosopher and the Chinese sage here merely as a point of departure for further exploration.) If we define strategists as those who conatively attune themselves to the immediate field of influences in which they are immersed, then we can say that strategists are concerned not with idealizations of reality but with their own immediate situation and how the influences at play in it are impinging, corporeally and tangibly, on their agency. (The word 'strategy' derives from the Greek *strategia*, 'office or command or art of a general', from *stratos*, 'multitude, army, expedition' and *agein*, 'to lead, guide, drive, carry off', from Sanskrit *ajirah*, 'moving, active'.[2]) One does not need

---

2 See Online Etymology Dictionary, https://www.etymonline.com/word/strategy. Also *World Book Dictionary* (1972), Doubleday: Chicago.

a theory about the underlying nature of reality in order to respond strategically to this field: one can feel the environmental pressure increasing and decreasing as one responds now this way, now that. Nor is there any sense of this world as a circumscribed totality; it extends just as far as the range of one's own sensitivity. As one moves around in it this range is constantly changing. To train the strategic faculty, one does not teach discursive rules of truth-making but rather sets exercises or practices which increase sensitivity and responsiveness. Chinese sages typically received their training in martial, meditative and other Daoist arts rather than in abstract speculation: where philosophers theorized, sages *cultivated*.

Although the sage is not setting out to arrive at truth, after the fashion of the philosopher, he does quickly discover, through his attitude of strategic engagement, that the best way of negotiating the immediate field of influences in which he is immersed – where this field includes the cross-cutting wills or conativities of others – is generally to adapt to them. The best way of negotiating such a field, in other words, is to make one's own ends as consistent as possible with surrounding influences and conativities, rather than seeking to impose oneself upon them. This is self-evident, as explained in Lecture 2, inasmuch as whoever achieves their goals in ways best calculated to conserve their own energy will, other things being equal, generally be most fit to continue to preserve and increase their own existence. By adopting the strategic path, the sage discovers these twin principles of conativity and accommodation/least resistance viscerally, within his own person. What he discovers, in other words, through practices of attunement to the forces and influences already at play in his environment, is Law.

The Way of Law: *Wuwei*

Not coincidentally, Law in this sense resonates strongly with the ancient Chinese notion of Dao or Way. Daoism is the Indigenous tradition of China, rooted in earlier shamanic traditions of the pre-agrarian societies that antedated Chinese civilization (Kohn 2017). Dao, translated as Way, is understood within this tradition as the spontaneous, generative Way of reality when things are left to their own devices. As one of the earliest source texts for Daoism, the *Yijing* (dating back to the eleventh century BCE), explains, 'the law of movement along the line of least resistance … [is] the law for natural events and for human life' (Wilhelm 1964: 67).

This resonance between Law and Dao emerges particularly clearly when we consider the cardinal Daoist modality of *wuwei*. *Wuwei* translates literally as non-action (*wu* meaning no- or non-; *wei* meaning action), but non-action is generally interpreted not as passivity or quietude but as action that is taken with rather than against the grain of things: one 'goes with the flow', carves with rather than against the grain of the block of wood or stone, surfs the waves rather than seeking mastery over them. Zhuangzi, in another source text of Daoism, illustrates *wuwei* via the story of an old man who falls into a river and is carried by the rapids to emerge downstream unscathed, having rolled with the waves and currents rather than resisting them, trusting that they will bring him to shore (Hamill and Seaton 1999). *Wuwei* is clearly then in some sense a modality of least resistance.

In the vast corpus of Daoist commentary, different interpretations of *wuwei* abound, but Daoism itself is adaptive: throughout its long history it has continually accommodated new historical circumstances. The fact that it can do so – the fact that its meaning is never exhausted within a particular historical context – is evidence of its profundity. Today then it behoves us to read *wuwei* against the background of environmental emergency. To do so is illuminating; it immediately suggests *wuwei* as a modality of synergy, a path of conativity whereby practitioners seek their own ends through accommodating the ends of others. As a strategy, this means deferring to elemental and organic tendencies, forces and energies – including conativities – already at play in one's environment, at least to the extent that doing so does not irremediably diminish one's own existence. But it also means harnessing those forces and energies to one's own conative cause, thereby saving oneself unnecessary exertion, while at the same time adjusting one's desires so that in fulfilling them one helps to create the conditions for the flourishing of others. To follow this path of accommodation and least resistance wisely then is to adapt, but selectively: one lets go of contingent ends and desires in order to encourage and support others who, in pursuit of their desires, will help to create optimal conditions for one's own self-preservation and self-increase (Mathews 2006).[3]

Around this core modality, discovered as a rule of action by the sage as he seeks to live effectively in his immediate environment, the outlines of a cosmology do intuitively take shape. But this is not a cosmology of the mind, a manifold spread out for the mental gaze, in the manner of theory, but a how-to cosmology of Dao, discovered and stored in the attuned body in the course of its responsive interactions with other bodies, other conativities. It is, in other words, a cosmology based not on theoretical postulates but on the sage's visceral experience as a practitioner of strategic arts. Evoked in early Daoist texts such as the *Daodejing* and the *Zhuangzi*, as well as the proto-text,

---

3 In a recent scholarly commentary on *wuwei*, *Daoism and Environmental Philosophy* (2021), Eric Nelson offers an interpretation of *wuwei* as 'responsive attunement', which resonates with the present account.

the *Yijing*, Dao is a way of *qi* or energy flow. The elements of nature (the 'Ten Thousand Things') are patterns in this flow. Such patterns form and re-form endlessly under the influence of the patterns forming and re-forming around them. When the Ten Thousand Things are left to arise spontaneously in this manner, under the mutual influences of one another, the universe assumes *its* own proper pattern or form – it follows *its* proper course.[4]

The patterns that Dao spontaneously constellates are comparable to those observable in water or indeed in any field of energy. Such patterns are always graceful and beautiful and somehow effortless, regardless of what distur-bances or obstacles are introduced into the field of flow. This is because such flows always follow the lines of least resistance. Water flows downhill. It fills the lowest places first. It flows around obstacles rather than trying to sur-mount them. If trapped it waits patiently until an opening occurs and then it starts to flow again. It makes no judgements or discriminations about where it will go. It just goes where the going is easiest. (This is a theme to which the *Yijing* returns again and again: 'it flows on and on, and merely fills up all the places through which it flows; it does not shrink from any dangerous spot nor from any plunge, and nothing can make it lose its own essential nature. It remains true to itself under all conditions' (Wilhelm 1964: 115)). Water makes no effort, which is why the idea of flow is equated with effortlessness. Flowing into whatever spaces are available, finding a way around obstacles rather than contending with them, insisting on nothing, but nevertheless, by dint of continuous adaptation to whatever presents, unwaveringly achieving its end, the river makes its way down to the sea. In wending its way thither and thereby achieving a destination proper to its nature, it simultaneously assists others in achieving their ends, sustaining the entire landscape with its waters, giving life to all things. 'Doing nothing' then, the river ensures that everything is done, that its work of sustaining the world is accomplished. (As Laozi observes, 'the thousands of things depend on it for life, it rejects nothing

---

4 'Underlying the *Yijing* philosophy of change is the notion that the cosmos is an organis-mic process without beginning or end. As a process, the cosmos resembles a great flow in which 'all of the parts of the entire cosmos belong to one organic whole' and all the parts 'interact as participants in one spontaneously self-generating process' (Tu 1985: 35). As such, there are three characteristics of this great flow: continuity, wholeness, and dynamism. It is continuous because it never stops in renewing itself. It is holistic because it includes everything in the universe and permeates in all aspects of life. It is dynamic because it is full of motion and movement, generating energy and strength all the time (Tu 1985: 38–39). In this cosmic flow, there is no distinction between the fol-lowing: the natural realm and the human realm, an observing subject and an observed object, and the inner world and the outer world. Everything is part of a totality, a group dance that never stops.' (Hon 2019)

... . It clothes and feeds the thousands of things, but does not act the ruler' (Lafargue 1992: 138).

The Daoist principle of action, *wuwei*, may then be seen to resonate, in Chinese thought, with the notion of Law, as understood in terms of the twin principles of conativity and accommodation/least resistance. In ecological contexts we may invoke this likeness by describing living things as following *wuwei* when they desire what others in their environment need them to desire. So, to return to our bettong, the little Australian marsupial introduced in Lecture 2, we might recall that bettongs desire truffles and other fungus. By digging into the forest floor to find these delicacies, bettongs nourish the soil in a variety of ways while also creating other conditions conducive to plant growth. Bettong activity in this sense helps to ensure the health of the forest that sustains bettong existence. As long as bettongs want what the forest needs them to want, nothing more is required of them but to follow their own desires: the forest will take care of them. This seems like a classic instance of *wuwei*. However, if a bettong wanted, not truffles but, say, cookies, it would have to go to extraordinary lengths to procure them, perhaps decamping to distant rubbish dumps on the peripheries of human settlements. Such exertion would deplete the bettong's energy. It would be counter to *wuwei*. And because the desire for cookies would divert the bettong away from its digging activities, its woodland ecosystem would likely also languish. The continued existence of both bettong and woodland would be jeopardized.

As already noted, the sage discovers *wuwei* not by theorizing but by cultivating his capacity for acuity and responsiveness in relation to his own immediate environment. What he discovers for himself, in his own person, will also, he reasons, be the case for others: *wuwei* must be a natural modality for other beings. What works for him as an agent, negotiating a field of environmental forces, is bound to work for other beings also strategically negotiating such fields. Hence *wuwei* is a strategy that, other things being equal, will be naturally selected for all.

In this sense, strategy as a way of knowing can reveal a holistic aspect of reality unattainable via theory. It does not offer us a 'view' of reality spread out for our epistemic gaze but rather insight into the *how-to* of reality – how as beings we are to live and thrive. This, as it turns out, is also consistent with Daoist teaching. The cosmology whereby Daoists sought to make intuitive sense of their strategic experience foregrounds not only the concept of *qi* but also that of *li*, which is in turn understood in terms of *yin* and *yang*. *Qi* is, as we have seen, generally translated as energy, but it is not energy in the physicist's sense, fully externalized in space and time. It is rather simply the currency of the dynamism that animates all things, grasped both inwardly, from the experience of one's own agency, and outwardly, through one's interactions with others. Under its never-ending changes, however, *qi*, as practitioners discover, conforms to *li*, or order: there is an inherent order in any manifestation of *qi*. This order is, as Alan Chan puts it, commenting on Wang Bi, an early neo-Daoist, 'marked by intelligible patterns and principles of operation … that can be described generally in terms of the interplay between the *yin* and *yang* vital forces'. This interplay of polarities in the never-ending outflow of *qi* ensures observable cycles such as those of the seasons or of growth and decay, as well as recurring but never exactly repeating patterns, such as those of the branches of trees (Chan 2019). It is this structuring principle of *li* which gives Dao its 'great constancy', according to Wang.

The play of *yin* and *yang*, like *qi* itself, also cannot be pinned down as equivalent to any of the externalizing categories of physics. Rather, the relation between *yin* and *yang* represents a self-correcting tendency in *qi* that assures its ongoingness: extremes of movement or dynamism in one direction will in due course self-correct in favour of the opposite direction, thereby preventing self-obliteration of the system. In this respect *qi* may be interpreted in terms of cosmo-conativity, the primordial thrust towards self-existence, while *yin/yang* polarity, as the inherent logic that shapes *qi* in accordance with the distinctive patterns of *li*, may be understood as the tendency on the part of finite things to realize themselves by accommodating one another and following paths of least resistance: the conative drive of individuals towards self-realization aligns with the forcefulness of *yang*, while their inclination to follow this drive by accommodating rather than resisting, suggests the yielding tendency of yin.[5]

In the terms of this cosmology, then, reality is no longer apprehended as a totality of things in space and time – the externalized universe that awes us with its vastness and whose fabric we probe with both our microscopes and our spaceships. It is intuited rather in how-to terms, as the pattern that expresses itself through us and around us, and indeed through and around all beings, if and when they come into existence. From this perspective, then, the primal nature of reality is not spatiotemporal but consists in *li*, in Law, which may be endlessly instanced but never summed or aggregated.

Accordingly, we must seek to know reality not as a totality, spread out for our theoretical gaze, but somatically from within, via particular instances

---

5 In his recent wide-ranging book *The Pattern of Meaning*, Jeremy Lent draws on threads from Indigenous thought, Chinese philosophy and contemporary science, particularly systems theory, to provide a philosophical frame for a contemporary ecological paradigm, much as I am doing in this book. He offers a – basically fractal – interpretation of *li*, comparable in some respects with the one offered here. See Lent 2021: 79 ff. Also Lecture 4, this volume.

of its manifestation. Through instantiating its *li*, we shall grasp *li* not merely as *li*, but as Law – as binding us to it. In order to know Law truly as Law, in other words, it is not enough merely to apprehend it as a descriptive principle; we need to feel its psychic pull. *Li* must become internalized as our own will. Knowing in this strategic sense then entails being conatively affected: it involves *feeling*.

Knowing the World through Feeling

For a vivid contemporary account of strategic knowing that explicitly factors feeling into cognition, let us turn now from Daoist China back to Aboriginal Australia. After all, the Daoist arts of acuity, accommodation and adaptiveness merely represent the formalization of a way of knowing that was normal and widespread in pre-agrarian societies. In order to subsist in such societies, people needed to know their local environment not theoretically but in the flesh, in all its particularity – they needed to be acquainted with the plants and animals of the region, their habits, needs, preferences, idiosyncrasies, their relationships with one another, their histories. Landscape had to be approached intimately, its terrain, affordances, hazards, quirks of climate and seasonality, as familiar to people as the workings of their own families. This was no detached, subject/object exercise but a practice of attentiveness to the particular that was guided, like the responses of a martial artist, by vital investment in the known.

In order better to understand the depth of contrast between a way of knowing that inextricably implicates feeling and the theoretic way of knowing that originated as *theoria* in ancient Greece and now enjoys epistemological hegemony throughout the world in the form of science, let us first very briefly review how *theoria* evolved into, indeed found its apotheosis in, modern science.

In classical science – the science that defined itself through its distinctive experimental, metrical and mathematical method in the seventeenth century – the dualist subject-object split that originated in *theoria* became externalized, explicit and institutionalized as the very hallmark of scientific method. As a condition for *objectivity* in its findings, science required *value-neutrality* on the part of the investigator. According to this requirement, the investigator must, if he is to avoid projecting his desires, prejudices and preconceptions onto the object of inquiry, bracket his own ends, emotions and expectations, attend only to impersonal evidence, strictly follow self-evident rules of inference, and let the investigation lead to its own logical conclusion. The scientific knower must, in other words, step back from the object of inquiry, adopting the stance of a 'detached observer' with respect to it, lest the object sway his investigation by seeking to establish a direct agentic or communicative connection with him. In pre-empting any engagement or communicative overture on the part of the object, while also withholding any response or overture of his own, the scientific knower thus prevents any relationship of an affective kind – whether positive or negative – from intruding into the inquiry.

Such a stance of detached neutrality is commendable inasmuch as it does prevent unintentional bias, intentional ideological distortion and emotional attachment from warping knowledge. But it also implies that the knower thus assumes, for the purposes of the inquiry, a tacitly solipsist stance, the stance of a lone subject in a world of 'objects', objects that are effectively 'ex-communicated' by the rules of the inquiry. Scientific method, in other words, enacts, by its very rules, an affective gap between knower and known, a gap that rigorously divorces feeling from cognition.

It is not surprising then that societies ideologically rooted in science, as modern industrial societies are, implicitly occupy a solipsist stance with respect to the object-realms posited by their institutionalized scientific practices. In the nineteenth century, these object-realms included not only fauna and flora and indeed the whole of nature but, notoriously, Indigenous peoples as well, who were studied – observed, examined, measured, dissected – in exactly the same way as were fauna. In the twenty-first century this object-realm, as posited by science, no longer includes Indigenous peoples but continues to include fauna and flora and the rest of nature, which are accordingly treated in brutally instrumentalist fashion. Such a solipsist stance is the end-point of a form of cognition completely divorced from feeling. It can therefore in no way reveal to the knower the normative pull of Law.

For an alternative – strategic – conception of knowledge that ties cognition to feeling, let us turn to three Senior Aboriginal Lawmen (SLM): Bill Neidjie, from Kakadu in the Northern Territory and David Mowaljarlai from the Kimberley in Western Australia, whose 'oratories' have been insightfully interpreted by Indigenous scholar Christine Black; and Paddy Roe, also from the Kimberley, who entrusted his non-Indigenous colleague, Frans Hoogland, with aspects of his legacy. The testimony of these Senior Lawmen conveys an epistemological alternative that may be found, albeit in varying forms, in other Aboriginal societies around Australia.

Neidjie, Mowaljarlai and Roe all emphasize that Aboriginal ways of knowing cannot be extricated from *feeling*. Drawing particularly on an 'oratory' left by Bill Neidjie, *Story about Feeling*, Black explains how one comes to know the land and its beings not by adopting a stance of detached observation with respect to them, but by cultivating a sense of intimacy and partnership with them. Rather than stepping back from land, as the scientific observer does, Neidjie urges the knower actively to *address* land and its beings, acknowledging affinity and seeking collaboration with them. As Black says, 'the land-centredness of Aboriginal culture is not based on reason or theory, faith or scriptural authority, but on feeling' (Black 2011: 41). She quotes Hannah Bell, longtime student of SLM Mowaljarlai: 'you must suspend your more familiar intellectual thinking in favour of sensory receptivity, awareness, and responsiveness. Above all, you must observe nature mindfully, listen to the elements carefully and receive knowledge subjectively' (Black 2011: 23–24).

To receive knowledge subjectively in this sense is not to project one's own emotion onto the known but to attend to it empathically, with an expectation of the possibility of relationship, of intimacy, of a certain kind of interior access. It is, in a word, to receive knowledge through feeling. Responsive attentiveness to the ecological patterns as well as to the minutiae of one's local surroundings gives rise, in the languages of the Kimberley, to a capacity for cognitive feeling known as *liyan* – a visceral way of knowing that is shared not only by people but by all beings and by land itself. Frans Hoogland, in dialogue with Paddy Roe, explains *liyan* as follows.

In order to experience [this feeling], we have to *walk the land*. At a certain time for everybody, the land will take over. The land will take that person. You think you're following something, but the land is actually pulling you. When the land starts pulling you, you're not even aware you're walking – you're off, you're gone. When you experience this, it's like a shift of your reality. You start seeing things you never seen before. I mean, you're trained one way or other and you actually look through that upbringing at the land. ... And all of a sudden, it doesn't fit anything. Then something comes out of the land, guides you. It can be a tree, a rock, a face in the sand, a bird ... . Then another thing might grab your attention, and before you know it there's a path created that is connected to you. It belongs to you, and that is the way you start to communicate with the land, through your path experiences. And that path brings you right back to yourself. You become very aware about yourself. You start to tune finer and finer. Then you become aware that when you're walking the path, it's coming out of you – you are connected to it ... [When this happens] we get a shift in mind that drops down to a feeling. Then we wake up to feeling, what we call le-an [*liyan*] here, and we become more alive, we start feeling, we become more sensitive. You start to read the country ... Then you wake up, ... and the country starts living for you. Everything is based on that feeling le-an [*liyan*], seeing through that feeling. (Sinatra and Murphy 1999: 19–21) (my italics)[6]

To experience the land's responsiveness to one's own presence in this organic way cannot leave one other than profoundly moved: to sense that one is noticed and intimately acknowledged by land is to experience a metaphysical affirmation that anchors one's existence in a level of reality that lies beyond the ordinary. Although this experience is subjective, in the sense that it relies on *interpretation* of communicative cues – as indeed does all communication – it may involve a self-evidence at the level of affect that will render it resistant to scepticism: just as 'seeing is believing', so is feeling, properly understood, believing. It is this kind of feeling – a blend of sensory attunement, somatic resonance, conative investment and even a sense of entry into the inner life of the cosmos – that is generally so absent in the scientific experience of the world. Once such a way of knowing-through-feeling has been discovered, however, there can be no question of relegating one's environment to some object-realm exclusively defined – and thereby disenfranchised – by theory. Slipping under the subject-object divide by way of cognitive feeling implicates land in one's own being. One will, in the words of Anne Poelina and her Indigenous and non-Indigenous co-authors, have 'become family with it' (Poelina et al. 2020; Wooltorton et al. 2020b). Land, under this aspect, is perceived as Country, in the distinctive Aboriginal sense. 'Country is living, responsive and caring, and [the word] is capitalised to denote an Indigenous understanding of one's place, which connects people, socio-economic systems, language, spirit and Nature through interrelationship' (Wooltorton et al. 2020a). The upshot of the shift from knowing as an outsider, the traditional Western stance, to becoming family with Country, knowing it as an insider through feeling, is that we discover that if we have love for Country, 'Country will have love for us'.

Knowing-through-feeling emanates from an underlying orientation that takes *relationship* for granted as the basic condition for life. Relationship is a precondition for the feeling that in turn orients one to one's world. Through feeling, as Neidjie explains, the knower is able to sense in his own body to what extent his immediate environment is in or out of balance. Balance is understood as a dynamic and continuous process of restoring symmetry between competing forces in a field of energies, energies representative of the distinct

---

6 In his recent book, *Total Re-Set*, Greg Campbell, an associate of SLM Paddy Roe and Hoogland, details many conversations with Lulu (Roe) and Hoogland on the topic of *liyan*. (Campbell 2022)

but related components of the environment. Each of these components has its own conative trajectory but at the same time must, if the system is to remain generative for life, allow its trajectory to be adapted in response to conative pressures from without. The conative trajectories of distinct components must remain mutually responsive and co-adaptive in this way if relationship is to be preserved: unbalanced relationships result ultimately in the collapse of distinction between parties and hence in the collapse of relationship itself. Relationship in the relevant sense then requires an ongoing stance of active accommodation with respect to others who are at the same time acknowledged as autonomous centres of self-activity (Black 2011; Rose 1992; Graham 2019; Mathews 2020).

In Aboriginal societies, this insight into relationship as a condition for feeling and hence for knowing, and of balance as a condition for ongoing relationship, functions, as we have seen, as a root intuition, articulated as Law, Law which is patterned into the fundamental structure of reality (Graham 2019). Whilst Law is storied in different ways across different Aboriginal nations within Australia, the underlying intuition remains that it is fundamentally a Law of Relationship (Black 2011; Graham 2019). The truth of this intuition is borne out at an empirical level by the evidence of inexhaustibly complex ecological inter-dependencies in local environments, but it is definitively revealed, as already noted, at a more somatic level, via the knower's capacity to feel in his own body the energies in the fields of relationships that surround him. This faculty of feeling, like other cognitive modalities in humans, may be cultivated or repressed by specific education systems or enculturation processes. In pre-agrarian societies such as those of Aboriginal Australia, it was cultivated via life-long practices of 'walking the land'. In many modern societies this faculty has been repressed in favour of the theoretic modalities emanating from science. But with appropriate training the student may gradually become so attuned to Country as not only to detect departures from Law in her immediate surrounds but become disposed herself to act spontaneously in accordance with Law, without need for external inducements or threat of penalties (Black 2011: 25).

In conclusion, we cannot access reality holistically, nor hence discern our proper human role in the cosmos, via theory. Theory can point us towards reality, descriptively, like the Buddhist finger pointing at the moon, but it cannot include us in the wholeness of the real; it cannot pull us into Law. In this sense, reality is not primordially extensional – extended in space and time – but intensional: it can be instanced, and its instances repeated endlessly albeit variably, each instance being unique to its particular context, but it can never be summed. Only by immersing ourselves directly, strategically, in reality as it is manifest to us under its always local aspect, by engaging responsively as attuned agent in a local field of cross-cutting conativities, can we channel *qi* through our person, thereby experiencing that feeling described in the Kimberley as *liyan* – our own *liyan* which is at the same time the *liyan* of the land, the living cosmos. To experience that feeling is already to be under the sway of Law, actualizing *li*. It is to have become a Lawful person, what Daoists call a Real Human, and perhaps what Aboriginal legal scholar Irene Watson is referring to when she speaks of the will to live in a place of lawfulness.

Today in the modern world the will to live in a place of lawfulness is lost to the greater humanity. Evidence of this is found in the growing list of global crises, poverty, environmental disasters, famine, war, and violence. What the greater humanity have come to know as law is a complex maze of rules and regulations; the body of law is buried, barely breathing. Law came to us in a song, it was sung with the rising of the sun, law was sung in the walking of the mother earth, law inhered in all things, law is alive, it lives in all things … Law was not imposed, and those who lived outside the law did just that, they were in exile from the law. We could say the greater proportion of humanity now lives in exile from the law. (Watson 2000: 4)

Lecture 4

DO WE NEED TO REINVENT PRAXIS TO CREATE AN ECOLOGICAL CIVILIZATION?

How Can We 'Walk the Land' in the Twenty-First Century? Pre-agrarian versus Post-agrarian Forms of Praxis

We have thus far considered the argument that in order to open ourselves up to the kind of holistic consciousness that divulges Law, we have not merely to devise new theories, such as animism or panpsychism, but adopt a different epistemic orientation – a strategic as opposed to a theoretic one. The strategic orientation arises out of specific forms of embodied, communicative and inter-conative practice, forms of practice indicated in Lecture 3 under the trope of 'walking the land'.

Walking the land, as understood in the Kimberley context, is not of course merely a recreational or sporting exercise, like modern-day hiking, orienteering or mountaineering, nor is it of purely therapeutic significance, as perhaps are the various martial and temple arts of Daoism. Land-based recreations and Daoist arts may indeed call, at their best, for a *wuwei* approach to one's environment, but walking the land, in the Kimberley sense, is closer to a form of *praxis*. I am using 'praxis' here in a basically Marxist sense to mean our core economic practices – the practices whereby particular societies, or groups within society, obtain their livelihood from their environment. (For Marx the concept of praxis was closely tied to that of *production*, where productive activity was understood by him as the kind of activity whereby we intentionally transform our environment to serve our own material purposes.[1] Here however I shall define it in terms of *provisioning*: praxis consists in the forms of activity whereby we intentionally act on or with our environment to provide

---

1 Interpretations of the Marxist notion of praxis abound. I am here following feminist political theorist, Alison Jaggar. (Jaggar 1984: 55).

for ourselves.) In speaking of 'walking the land', I take Senior Lawmen such as Mowaljarlai and Roe to mean, in other words, that one is walking it with a view, at least in part, to one's material sustenance, tending it that so it may in turn sustain oneself and one's people.

The pre-agrarian praxis of First Nations peoples such as Aboriginal Australians has often in the past been described as foraging or hunter-gathering, but this fails to convey the great variety of pre-agrarian societies around the world (Graeber and Windrow 2021). Traditional Australians were proactive in taking care of their country. While they did not replace pre-existing ecosystems with cultivated croplands or displace wildlife in order to pasture domesticated 'livestock', in the typical agrarian manner, they did systematically use regenerative-ecological techniques, such as firing and selective hand harvesting, to increase the productivity of land both for ecosystems and for humans (Gammage 2011; Pascoe 2014; Steffensen 2020). In other words, instead of imposing themselves on land by domesticating it, traditional Australians worked skilfully and knowledgeably with its conative grain, supporting that grain while adapting their needs to its affordances, thereby ensuring the ongoing flourishing of the wider system as well as their own flourishing.

We might describe this kind of regenerative praxis as the praxis of peoples who act not merely as hunters and gatherers passively living off the land, nor as farmers who domesticate it, but as *custodians* who work with its wild grain to ensure that it incidentally continues to provide for them. An axiom of such praxis is that a wealth of mutually adapted other species is required to sustain the specific subset of plant and animal species on which a society of custodians directly depends. It will ultimately be the ecosystem itself that does the work of providing for the people, but the people are careful to 'care for country' in everything they do, while nevertheless nudging it – by gently amplifying selected natural pressures already in train – to favour certain species over others, without net detriment to the system.[2]

Let us describe this form of praxis as a praxis of custodianship. (It seems best, at least initially, to avoid the adjective, 'custodial', since the major connotation of this term in popular usage often pertains to imprisonment.) Clearly the praxis of custodianship, according to the present account, is informed

---

2 While Aboriginal Australia offers many examples of ecological custodianship, such praxes are widespread around the world. Custodian societies do often include practices of hunting and gathering but they also actively biodiversify their estates, ensuring by their praxis that those estates remain rich terrains of life for a multitude of species (Graeber and Wengrow 2021; Maffi 2010).

with the twin principles of conativity and accommodation/least resistance, principles I have suggested converge with those underlying Aboriginal conceptions of *Law*. Custodians conform their lives to the unfolding of Law, guiding one another and their environments in accordance with it (Watson 2014; Black 2011; Rose 1992).

Nothing in such lives, guided by the ethos of custodianship, is conducive to a dualist outlook. For custodians, there are not, as there are for traditional farmers, two worlds, that of the human and that of nature, where the human is the enclosed world of cultivated field, hearth, house and meaning and therefore of communication, while nature is the wild world that lies beyond the circle of settlement, bereft of meaning for humans and hence beyond the reach of communication. Pre-agrarian reality is a single world, a world that is a seamless tapestry of both culture and nature, mind and matter, human and animal, conatively and communicatively intermeshed and incessantly engaged in exchanges of both flesh and meaning (Viveiros de Castro 1998). In the midst of this cosmos of cross-species multiculturalism, pre-agrarians are inalienably at home – 'inalienably', because there is nowhere and nothing outside their cosmos into which they might fall. There is thus, amongst such peoples, an existential groundedness – a literal sense of feeling at home around the open campfire, sitting empty-handed on the dirt, in the midst of the Milky Way. Such a sense of groundedness contrasts with a certain anxiety and 'search for meaning' that typifies life amidst the clutter and claustrophobia of agrarian societies. The anxious search for lost meaning is arguably what drives the impulse towards transcendence that finds expression in axial religions – religions such as Judaism, Christianity, Islam and Buddhism that originated in the agrarian era and persist into the present (Mathews 2017a).

While many custodian societies, such as those of Aboriginal Australia, have continued their praxes of custodianship to the present day, others, at different times in different parts of the world, transitioned to agriculture as their basic praxis. Often already adept at regenerative techniques of wild harvesting, such peoples started to settle into fertile areas where tubers, grains or other staples could be cultivated more intensively. Animals were domesticated for meat, milk, wool, fur, labour and transport. More intensive food production allowed for the expansion of permanent settlements into towns and cities. Production and storage of food surplus enabled social specialization: artisans together with military and religious workforces could be spared from the fields to dedicate themselves to specific services. The availability of food surpluses, together with the emergence of artisanry and eventually manufacture, also gave rise to possibilities of wealth and hence to social stratification and political hierarchy. Not all agrarian societies underwent such a series of transformations: village scale horti-culture persisted indefinitely in some areas and in some instances became so interwoven with local ecologies that local biodiversity, far from being depleted, was enriched by such praxis (Maffi 2010). Indeed, over the mil-lennia a wide variety of hybrid forms of praxis, combining agriculture with hunting, gathering and fishing, evolved. Nor was a degree of social speciali-zation absent from all societies organized around ecological custodianship (Graeber and Wendrow 2021). But where political hierarchy and ensuing centralization of political power did occur, they established foundations for the rise of cities and city-states, and, as an adjunct to the administrative functions of states, literacy and civil law. In other words, with the advent of agriculture all the elements of *civilization*, as descriptively understood, emerged and started to constellate.

Whatever the details of such typologies of societies – and they are cur-rently much in contention in scholarly circles – the suggestion here is that the further societies moved from pre-agrarian praxes towards the forms of agrarianism associated with the Fertile Crescent, involving land clearing and replacement of indigenous ecologies with crops and domesticated 'live-stock', the more people's experience became split into the two aforementioned spheres: (i) an exclusively human one, in which all that was wild, self-sustain-ing and self-regenerating was either replaced by human-built environments or domesticated to serve human ends, often with little or no consideration for the ecological effects of those interventions on the landscape at large; and (ii) the sphere of the wild, no longer intimately known or understood, no longer inhabited, construed merely as backdrop to the all-important human sphere. This divorce of agrarian societies from local ecologies marks the beginning of the consciousness that separates itself from nature, opting for an impose-and-control attitude rather than an attitude of accommodation. In this sense agrarianism represents the earliest departure from Law. The farmer clears the land rather than choosing to coexist with it. He builds his own environ-ment rather than dwelling within the affordances of the landscape. He erases the given in order to replace it with an abstractly premeditated alternative of his own. It is a long way from the early days of the Neolithic to ancient Greece, but we might recognize in agriculture the praxical origins of the human/nature dualism that found its definitive articulation in the theoretic consciousness of early Greek thought.

In some parts of the world a cultural memory of the unitive cosmos was preserved even as societies became progressively agrarianized. This was arguably the case in ancient China. Although Chinese society was fully agrarian by the time early Daoist texts began to appear in the fourth century BCE, the shift towards agriculture having begun circa 6000 BCE, the much older notion of Dao itself was, as we have seen, deeply resonant with the unitive cosmos of pre-agrarian cultures. While there might be many ways of explaining this vestige of pre-agrarian thinking in an agrarian society, one possibility is that it might have been due to the extraordinary cultural continuity of Chinese history. Though ethnically diverse, the societies of the proto-Chinese region of the Yellow River and Yangtze River basins seem not to have been subject to outright conquest or colonization by foreigners. Even during later imperial periods of 'barbarian' (Manchu and Mongol) domi-nance, Chinese language was maintained as the language of governance; Manchus and Mongols themselves were significantly Sinicized rather than subsuming the Chinese under their own foreign cultures. This continuity might account for a carry-over of culture in the area, particularly in the shape of shamanism, from pre-agrarian to agrarian societies. Shamanism was co-opted by early rulers to legitimate social and political hierarchiza-tion (Kohn 2017). With its roots in totemism, and hence in identification with the energies and diverse conativities of nature, shamanism brought into the imperial order imprints of the pre-agrarian, holistic sensibility via the archaic trope of Dao (where this was of course a root trope of Chinese civi-lization long before the emergence of 'Daoism' as a distinct set of teachings). No such cultural continuity existed between the pre-agrarian societies of Greece and those that succeeded them: the original territory that came to be known as Greece was subject to successive waves of conquest and coloniza-tion by alien pastoral peoples, probably from the Russian steppe (Mathews 2016). No trace of the Indigenous, pre-agrarian past accordingly lingered in the civilization that emerged in the classical era, leaving the way open for the full articulation of agrarian dualism that we find expressed in *philosophia*, and eventually in the theory-based consciousness that has overtaken the West by way of science.

A second important point in this connection is that though Daoism is indeed indigenous to China, it has functioned since its earliest days as a highly aestheticized tradition, more as a counterculture in fact than as a guide to everyday life. It tends to be avowed in the seclusion of the mountains rather than in the hustle and dust of the marketplace. Through the last two millen-nia, artists, poets, sages and thinkers have withdrawn to lofty Daoist retreats to reflect on metaphysical questions, free from the hubbub of civilization. Down in that hubbub, however, people have continued to strive relentlessly for material prosperity rather than dwelling in communion with Dao. Any excess of competitiveness and strife that prosperity as a goal might unleash in society was contained, not so much by appeal to the yielding influence of Dao as to the Confucian ethos of filial obedience to the patriarchal family and state. True, the rootedness of the Chinese psyche in an aesthetic of Dao may have shaped the trajectory of Chinese civilization, inclining it away from early uptake of mechanistic science and hard-edged technologies in favour of a more literary outlook. But on the ground and in the field, Daoism appears not to have tempered the impact of agrarianism on the land: the environmental history of China has, as Mark Elvin shows in his book, *The Retreat of the Elephants: an Environmental History of China*, generally been no better than that of other civilizations.[3]

To admit the countercultural status of the Daoist outlook in China is not to discount the potential of this outlook as a resource for social change in our present day. Dao remains a deep if subliminal root of Chinese identity. In this respect it is available to be culturally and politically mobilized: if the Chinese are encouraged to reclaim Dao as key to a new civilization ardently awaited around the world, they might willingly forge an alternative economic path to reach it. The consciousness of Dao can conceivably only be reinhabited in this way, however, if it shifts from its current status as a vestigial, aestheticized trope to a living experience, where this can happen, I would suggest, only if it is accessed via strategic practices of attentiveness, acuity and accommodation with respect to local environments.

Can Modern Mass Societies Develop a Strategic Orientation through Praxis?

But again, how could such strategic practices be re-launched in the contemporary world on a mass scale? Spiritual exercises such as those taught in Daoist temples, as well as lifestyle choices such as mountaineering, surfing or bird watching, might indeed be conducive to a strategic orientation at a personal level but would likely make little difference to the economic habits of society at large. But nor can humanity revert *en masse* to the traditional praxis of custodians – the praxis of 'walking the land'. Even were the biosphere not already in crisis and even were large numbers of modern people willing to take up such a traditional way of life – which they patently are not – the planet could not begin to support seven billion people living in accordance with those older ways.

---

3 In his book, *The Patterning Instinct,* Jeremy Lent offers a detailed account of the so-called Great Divergence between China and the West, particularly as regards the fact that China chose not to follow a path of scientific development despite the presence of many proto-scientific discoveries and inventions in its earlier history (Lent 2017). For a classic discussion, see Sivin 1982.

Bioregionalism

Are there then alternative modes of livelihood, applicable in a twenty-first century setting, that might bend societies back towards a strategic orientation and hence towards consciousness of Dao or Law? An optimal praxical scenario for recovering such consciousness would surely consist in a wholesale return of people to regimes of relative self-sufficiency: small scale production using regenerative and sustainable techniques of horticulture and manufacture adapted to local conditions and sensitive to local ecologies. In the West a grass-roots movement towards such a cultural and economic transition has been in existence for decades; it goes by the name of *bioregionalism*. Bioregionalism is a politics and practice that calls for devolution of the present global network of urbanized, politically centralized and stratified, highly extractive and ecologically disruptive economies based on mass production into a multitude of small, low-impact economies organized around relatively autonomous bioregional communities. A bioregion is, in environmental philosopher, Eileen Crist's, words, 'a geographical location characterized by a topography, animal and plant communities, soil types, bodies of water, weather patterns and microclimates, humidity and aridity gradients, animal migrations, human histories, and other unique histories' (Crist 2019: 231). Bioregionalism seeks to reconnect socially just human communities in a sustainable manner to the scale of the bioregions in which they are embedded (Aberley 1999: 13). Societies built on this model would substitute simpler, decentralized, ecologically sensitive and -literate, place-identified, value-rich but technically minimal and scale-appropriate forms of cultural and material life for current homogenized regimes of global distribution and consumption (Crist 2019; McGinnis 1999; Sale 1985). All praxis, in the bioregional scenario, is attuned to the unique ecology of place, where this in turn is generative both of culture and, across local societies and regions, of cultural differentiation.

Although the basic praxis in this scenario is agrarian, and to that extent may inherit the proto-dualizing tendency of agrarianism, the bioregionalist consciously seeks to revision farming along regenerative lines to render it as consistent as possible with ecological integrity. Such regenerative approaches to farming are currently proliferating and gaining a popular following around the world. These approaches include permaculture, ecological agriculture, restorative agriculture, natural sequence farming and holistic management, amongst others.[4] Practised in accordance with these new approaches, farm-

---

4 For permaculture, see the many works of Bill Mollison and David Holmgren; for ecological farming, Soule and Piper, 1992; for regenerative farming, Massy, 2017; for natural sequence farming, Andrews, 2014; for holistic management, Savory 2017.

ing may indeed draw people into intimate relationships with local ecologies, relationships that may prove conducive to knowledge of Law. Indeed, bioregionalism is explicit on this point: its practitioners are exhorted to 'reinhabit' place in the expectation that Indigenous consciousness – adapted to present-day conditions – will thereby be revived (Snyder 2013).

As a movement, then, bioregionalism surely represents a promising praxical pathway to consciousness of Law and hence to a contemporary form of ecological civilization. It is a feasible political choice for individuals or groups in wealthier nations and to that extent ought surely to figure more prominently in green political rhetoric and policy settings. It is also consistent, to a degree, with older farming traditions in many other parts of the world (King 2004). Political discourse accordingly needs to validate those traditional lifeways, as thinkers and activists such as Vandana Shiva and Luisa Maffi have long argued, rather than invalidating them as 'under-developed'. At the same time, however, it must be acknowledged that bioregionalism seems to fly in the face of current worldwide demographic trends towards 'development' – towards urbanization and ever-greater concentrations of industrial production and consumption. These trends are driven not only by corporate interests but by a widespread conviction, however misguided, that 'development' represents the best solution to poverty and disadvantage. Systemic transition towards bioregionalism would thus seem to require outright reversal of perceived political and economic necessities. Hoping for any such systemic transition might therefore appear, in the present geopolitical moment, unrealistic.

Larger-scale alternatives

So, while advocating for a politics of bioregionalism where feasible, and affirming it as a seedbed for further social transformation, let us also consider whether a change of praxis more consistent with current geopolitical realities might be envisaged. Can societies satisfy material demands and provide for themselves economically at scale in ways that nevertheless work synergistically with the energies and conativities of nature? In other words, can modes of provisioning that conform to Dao or Law be devised at a mass level rather than merely at the level of individual self-sufficiency? I think they can, though in devising the requisite praxes we shall find ourselves circling back, at a different level of system, to the localism that is core to bioregionalism.

The key to devising such praxes is again for societies to follow the *wuwei* example of ecological landscapers – those species which, in pursuing their own desires, increase the affordances of the landscape for other species. We have already noted how First Nations peoples in Australia traditionally used fire as a landscaping tool. Fire was already a natural and adaptive part of Australian ecologies inasmuch as lightning strikes had always sparked bushland fires. By discovering the ways of fire in intricate and always unique local landscapes, understanding the rotation cycles of different species of plant and the fire behaviours of myriads of animal species, the first Australians devised highly attuned techniques and calendars of selective burning that encouraged conditions favourable to their own staple resources. The result was not 'blanket fires', such as those later used by colonists to clear forests for introduced agriculture, but burns that gently trickled through the bush, revitalizing it while also modifying it in ways that were productive both for humans and for biodiversity. The key to this praxis was knowledge, not effort or force. The degree of exertion required on the part of the people was relatively minor, but the effects on the landscape and the resulting bounty were large-scale.

Can Large-scale Praxis Be Reformed along the Lines of Biosynergy? Case studies

In the context of praxis and for ease of expression, let us refer to this *wuwei* approach as biosynergy. I have defined biosynergy in terms of a mutuality of conativities that involves a degree of codetermination of the parties in question: each party desires what the other needs them to desire if each is to fulfil its conativity (Mathews 2011). Let us, in the remainder of this Lecture, consider some examples of praxis that conform to the pattern of biosynergy. I shall draw on several authors whose work points in this direction. These include Tim Flannery, Judith Schwartz, Michael Pawlyn and Sarah Ichioka, Sergey Zimov and Julia Watson. (For a greater wealth of case studies than can be covered here, I refer the reader to their inspiring texts.)

In relation both to the provision of food and the related question of climate change, it is not too difficult to find projects that demonstrate a biosynergy approach. A proposal by Tim Flannery, Chief at Australia's Climate Council, conjoins climate change mitigation with both large-scale food and fuel provision for human populations and major increases in marine biodiversity through re-afforestation of marine environments with kelp. If 9% of the ocean were afforested with kelp and other seaweed, according to a 2012 study from the University of the South Pacific, a vast amount – 53 billion tonnes – of CO_2 per year would be removed from the atmosphere. Further benefits of kelp afforestation would include the de-acidification of surrounding sea water and, in consequence, restoration of an ideal environment for shell growth and hence for shellfish – to the extent, according to Flannery, that kelp forests on the envisaged scale could support sustainable fisheries capable of yielding 200 kilograms of seafood per year, per person, for 10 billion people. Kelp itself also has value as feedstock, fertilizer and as a source of biogas, while other seaweeds are suitable for human consumption (Flannery 2017: 141).

Kelp re-afforestation requires only relatively minor human investment of effort to set up the necessary initial conditions. Arrays of ropes on which seaweed and shellfish such as mussels could grow would be floated a little below the surface of the ocean; from these ropes, baskets filled with other varieties of shellfish such as scallops and oysters would be suspended. Pipes would be needed to bring water up from the ocean depths to provide nutrient for the seaweed arrays, as would platforms of solar panels to power the harvesting of seafood as well as floating docks for ships to transport the harvest to ports. Once these conditions were in place, nature could get on with the job, so to speak, without further assistance from us: kelp afforestation is a largely nature-led strategy, a classic instance of the *wuwei* approach. It echoes a natural event that occurred fifty million years ago. Azolla, a fast-growing freshwater fern, spread rapidly and profusely across a land-locked Arctic sea. In doing so it sequestered so much carbon that it converted the then greenhouse climate to an icehouse one (Brinkhuis et al. 2006). The kelp scenario, though instigated by ourselves, might help in like dramatic fashion to temper our present-day climate extremes.

A large acquaculture and conservation estate in Spain, Veta la Palma, affords another instance of nature-led praxis. Its approach to food provision has been described as 'extensive' as opposed to 'intensive' or factory farming.[5] Extensive 'farming' consists in habitat restoration for a suite of indigenous wildlife that is then selectively harvested. At Veta la Palma some large-scale landscaping was initially undertaken to restore marshlands which had earlier been drained for cattle production; these marshlands have subsequently become, on the one hand, the largest waterfowl sanctuary in Europe and, on the other hand, a major commercially viable supplier of wild seafood. The huge populations of waterfowl – comprised of up to 250 species and numbering up to 600,000 individuals at times – maintain optimum habitat health and nutrition for saltwater life. Instead of regarding birds as competitors for fish, the Veta La Palma team sees them, in classic *wuwei* style, as allies, as ecological assistants helping to do the hard work of maintaining conditions conducive to fish flourishing.

Another possibility for a *wuwei* approach to food provision in a country like Australia, which suffers major degradation from feral animal populations, would consist simply in harvesting the animals as meat for human consumption, in the process solving the ecological problem. Although limited

5 See <https://www.vetalapalma.es/en/extensive-aquaculture>

harvesting for the petfood market and for foreign export already occurs, feral meats – goat, camel and rabbit, for example – remain conspicuous by their absence from the Australian diet. Instead, further ecological damage is incurred, on an even larger scale, to deliver traditional but exotic domestic animals – sheep, chickens and cattle – to the table (Mathews 2011c). Australians have not to date been prepared to adjust their tastes and thereby, even to this minor degree, adapt to the needs of the continent's ailing ecosystems.

To advocate such an intervention in a categorical manner however is to miss the ecological nuance that is necessary for the practice of biosynergy. Increasingly it is recognized that in some environments under some circumstances, feral populations can contribute to land repair and biodiversity recovery. In the Kimberley in northwestern Australia, for example, government-led feral eradication programmes have, over the last 35 years, culled half a million feral donkeys. Yet as Judith Schwartz reports in her book *The Reindeer Chronicles*, a Kimberley pastoralist, paying close attention to the effects of donkey grazing on his estate, discovered that such grazing was resulting in wildfire mitigation and resurgence of vanished perennial ground-cover. Consistently with such findings, some researchers argue that exotic species such as donkeys, horses and camels can fill ecological niches vacated by now-extinct megafauna from the Pleistocene. Biologists argue that the worldwide loss of the teeming Pleistocene megafauna has left major ecological deficits in many landscapes – deficits that the reintroduction of equivalent modern species might redress. The recent emergence of this idea of 'megafauna rewilding' demonstrates that judgements regarding blanket interventions, such as culling, must be guided by intimate understanding of the various species in question, even of particular populations of those species, and of their multifaceted roles in local biosocial communities. Such judgements must in other words be informed not merely with theoretical knowledge but with high levels of on-the-ground ecological attentiveness and a feeling for the conative grain of particular landscapes.

In relation to climate change, Schwartz – following scientists, such as Michal Kravcik and his Slovakian team (Kravcik 2007), whose voices have found little traction in the policy mainstream – argues that the current perception of climate change as predominantly an effect merely of greenhouse gas emissions is too narrow, encouraging a correspondingly narrow, techno-oriented response that consists merely in retrofitting industry and energy systems along zero emissions lines while also devising ad hoc geo-engineering defences against radiation, fire, flood and drought.[6] Schwartz advocates a

---

6 To Kravcik et al, Schwartz might have added visionary Australian soil scientist, Walter Jehne, who has also long been advocating biological/hydrological approaches

more ecological approach to the problem. Climate instability is as much a result of disturbances to the hydrological cycle, the dying and desiccation of soils and the related loss of biomass and biodiversity, as it is of carbon emissions. The best way of addressing these aspects of the problem is by restoring ecological systems: desiccated soils must be allowed to rehydrate if they are to become biologically reactivated, where such reactivation increases their porosity and absorbancy and thus further boosts their capacity to rehydrate. Rehydration allows for further revegetation and hence sequestering of carbon, where such recarbonization increases soil fertility, and hence the capacity for revegetation, and so on, recursively. Well-hydrated, revegetated landscapes induce local rainfall and thereby help to stabilize climate locally and perpetuate hydration. The best 'tools' for achieving such ecosystem restoration are not merely the conventional conservation methods of direct seeding and weeding but the reintroduction of missing animal species, especially ecosystem engineers. In earlier lectures we noted how the foraging activities of ecological 'landscapers' like the 'little diggers' of Australia – species such as bettongs and lyrebirds – condition soils in ways conducive to optimal hydration. Large grazing ruminants are also prime vehicles of ecosystem repair. Megafaunal guts, Schwartz observes, act as giant, moist, roving incubating vats that break down nutrients and distribute them in a more assimilable state – along with seeds – across the landscape, thereby enhancing soil fertility and promoting revegetation (Schwartz 2020: 116).

One glorious example of wildlife-led recovery from global warming, also discussed by Schwartz amongst others, is the reintroduction of megafauna to the arctic tundra for the purpose of slowing permafrost melt. At their northern Siberian reserve, Pleistocene Park, the famous father and son team, Sergey and Nikita Zimov, are attempting to recreate, in microcosm, the Mammoth Steppe ecosystem with a view to reversing the processes that are causing arctic permafrost currently to melt at perilous rates. Permafrost melt is one of the factors considered most likely to trigger runaway warming, possibly in the near future, since it entails the thawing of thousands of years' worth of frozen vegetation stored in arctic soils. As the thawed vegetation decomposes, it releases vast quantities of greenhouse gases. By re-introducing long-gone megafaunal herbivores such as musk ox, reindeer, moose, bison and the Yakutian horse to the reserve, the Zimovs have shown that in grazing the tundra, herbivores trample down and thin snow cover that otherwise insulates the ground throughout winter. Unblanketed by snow, ground remains

---

to climate change. For an introduction to his work, see <https://www.regenerate-earth .org/library>.

frozen – permafrost is preserved. The Zimovs have measured a 15 degree Celsius difference between grazed and ungrazed winter soils (Schwartz 2020: 104). Grazing and browsing also prevent the 'shrubification' of the tundra, where woody vegetation – consisting of bushes and small trees – darkens the landscape and so absorbs more sunlight than does open, grassy vegetation, leading to greater warming. Re-establishing the Mammoth Steppe by restoring lost herbivores across the tundra could have global-scale effects on climate without the need for humanity to lift a finger.

All such wildlife-led or Earth-led projects, duly sensitized to locality and context, might be viewed as large-scale, twenty-first century analogues of custodianship, instances of a biosynergy approach to praxis. As one of Schwartz's interlocuters puts it, in making the point that the key to the climate is soil, and that the key to recharging the soil is to work with natural processes: 'Let the animals and nature do more of the work' (Schwartz 2013: 26).

Having sampled several instances of biosynergy in relation to food provision and climate recovery, let us now turn to the field of infrastructure and planning. Just as a kelp-led climate recovery relies basically on a simple system of ropes and baskets, so one of my favourite examples of a *wuwei* approach to planning is the ancient Dujiangyang Irrigation Scheme, established in 256 BCE on the Min River in the Chinese province of Sichuan. The system was built to protect local people from the dangerous annual flooding of the river. Instead of constructing a *dam* that would literally *block* the flow of the river, the Daoist governor at the time, Li Bing, devised a series of channels, held in place by bamboo baskets filled with stones, that harmlessly and productively dispersed the waters across the plain, making that flood plain the richest agricultural area in China. In contrast to the massive dams that were an unfortunate hallmark of China's 'scientific' development in the latter half of the twentieth century, the Dujiangyan system does not damage the ecology of the river, even though it reconfigures it: fish and other aquatic life have free passage through the system. Where dams generally succumb to ecological death and silt-up in a matter of decades, and are thought to contribute to geological instability, Dujiangyan is still as benignly functional and productive today as it was more than two thousand years ago, and it emerged almost unscathed from the catastrophic Sichuan earthquake of 2008 (Watts 2010).

For a comparable contemporary example of infrastructure from a biosynergy perspective, let us turn to a chemical-free waste-water treatment plant in India. There, on the outskirts of Kolkata, a large network of channels and pools, flanked by freeways and mountains of smoking garbage, receives 7 million litres of raw sewage each day. Over a period of several months, the waste-water passes through a series of pre-treatment sedimentation and oxidation ponds, after which it is released into a system of shallow pools where waste is broken down under the action of sunlight, algae and bacteria while simultaneously feeding a large fish population, which in turn becomes a food source for the city. Thirteen thousand tonnes of fish per year are supplied by fishermen to local markets. Before the water enters the Bay of Bengal, it fertilizes the city's rice fields and other agricultural lands. A rich diversity of wild plant and fish life is also supported by these working wetlands (Watson 2020: 323 ff).

Is there a distinction between biosynergy and biomimicry?

In the spheres of architecture and manufacture, examples of a biosynergy approach are harder to come by. While there is no shortage of innovators influenced by the design school of *biomimicry*, a distinction between biomimicry and biosynergy is generally not observed. As a design philosophy, biomimicry is associated with thinkers such as biologist Janine Benyus, architect William McDonough and economists Amory and Hunter Lovins. Benyus defines biomimicry as 'a new science that studies nature's models and then imitates or takes inspiration from these designs and processes to solve human problems, eg a solar cell inspired by a leaf'. She adds that biomimicry is also 'a new way of viewing and valuing nature. It introduces an era based not on what we can *extract* from the natural world, but on what we can *learn* from it' (Benyus 2002, front pages).

All manner of commodities, buildings and technologies are currently being produced or proposed in accordance with biomimicry design principles. Examples, cited by Benyus and others, include the original instance of biomimicry, the self-fastening fabric, Velcro, designed in 1948 by a Swiss engineer who observed, when brushing his dog, the mechanism by which burrs clung to the dog's fur; a 'smart' clothing fabric composed of 'scales', which open in warm conditions and close in cold conditions, where this fabric is modelled after pine cones, which likewise open and close according to temperature; external paints that, once applied, are self-cleaning, modelled after the lotus leaf, the bumpy molecular surface structure of which is such that dirt particles cannot stick but are rolled off by rain drops; buildings which imitate the structure of termite mounds in order to cool themselves, termite mound temperature being maintained at a constant 87 degrees Fahrenheit by an internal chimney effect, so that funguses can be farmed by the termites inside the mounds; fabric that can be stuck to furniture and easily peeled off when in need of replacement, the adhering mechanism being inspired by geckos, whose foot pads adhere to surfaces without glue, using small doses of static electricity (Mathews 2011).

But biosynergy, as I understand it here, is not a design principle. It does not ask for self-cleaning paints or peelable furniture fabric. Such innovations fail the biosynergy test and indeed miss the entire point of biosynergy. After all, the systematic redesign of all our manufacture, architecture and engineering along biomimetic lines could result in a wholly human-made but nevertheless fully self-sustaining world built in accordance with circular, no-waste operating principles found in nature. Though such a manufactured world would *imitate* natural systems at a design level, thereby perhaps avoiding pollution, resource exhaustion, global warming and other systemic threats to human viability, it might in no way *synergize* with those original systems, but might rather replace them altogether with human-made systems of its own (Mathews 2011). While this was in no way the intention of thinkers such as Benyus, it is a possible outcome of an ambiguity at the heart of the notion of mimicry or imitation. One might imitate a pattern not for the purpose of accommodating but of appropriating. The ancient Romans, for example, imitated the genius of the Etruscans in the design of many aspects of their own civilization, but this was not a case of accommodation; on the contrary, the Romans imitated the Etruscans all the better to annihilate them and erase them from history.

Biosynergy however avoids this ambiguity: it represents not a design principle but a *protocol* – a protocol for *engaging* with a world which is already alive with dispositions, meanings, values and agendas of its own. The concept of design itself is, from a biosynergy perspective, somewhat suspect, as premised on theoretic thinking: the designer abstracts the underlying mechanisms that account for functionality in living systems then re-applies them in the service of arbitrary human ends. The traditional designer's 'blueprint' for a commodity or system is very much a variant of the scientist's 'theory': it is a schema or calculus that lays out in preconceived, abstract, metrical terms how to build the prospective object or system and itemizes the materials required to produce it. The concept of design would need to be much expanded beyond this blueprint model if it were to be understood as basically referring to protocol.

The starting point for a biosynergy approach in the spheres of manufacture and architecture, then, is not the question, how shall we model X on some natural mechanism; it is rather the question of whether the desire for X is itself a synergistic desire. Is X something that other members of our ecological communities need us to want? This is not quite the same as the question biomimicry designer, William McDonough, asks in relation to the production of a hair gel: what does the river into which that hair gel will eventually be discharged want of this product, where McDonough is anticipating answers like 'a pollution-dispersing agent'. (McDonough and Braungart 2002) From a biosynergy perspective we ask rather, what does that river need us to want in the first place? What does a river want from its people if it is to thrive as a river and continue to support its human and wider-than-human communities?

If we take this question seriously, the desire for hair gel and other such commodities is likely to fade away altogether. What a river, a living cosmos, wants of its people may be not pollution-dispersing agents but an entire culture of communicative and conative engagement, whereby our sense of our own meaning and purpose becomes suffused with the meanings that the river, as part of the living cosmos, has for itself. Unless we address this larger question of what the river or the larger ecological community needs us to want, we will never achieve the synchrony of conativities that will enable us to live within Law. A bettong – to return to our earlier story – who wanted cookies rather than truffles and ventured out of its native woodlands to get them might dutifully return to the woodlands to defecate, thereby enriching the woodland soil. But its failure to dig for truffles would nonetheless impact the woodland ecology in a myriad of other ways. If moreover other woodland dwellers, such as bilbies, bandicoots, kowaris, quolls and sticknest rats, also developed idiosyncratic tastes, then no matter how much they tried to compensate for consequent deviations from their regular ecological roles – by devising their own equivalents of 'pollution-dispersing agents' – the synchrony of conativities that assures the ongoing integrity of the ecosystem could never be achieved.

Piecemeal redesign of arbitrary commodities, in short, will not add up to a self-regenerating ecosystem. Our desires, as humans – and hence the kinds of commodities we choose to produce – must mesh systemically with the needs and desires of other species. This requires flexibility on our part. We remain committed, as organisms, to fulfilling our own conativity, but we must be flexible in respect of means – in response to the affordances of particular environments. If the kelp re-afforestation scenario, for example, is to succeed, markets would have to be prepared to switch staples from meat to seafood. Likewise, if the harvesting of feral animals for human consumption were in some circumstances to prove ecologically productive in Australia, traditional food preferences would, as we have noted, need to become responsive to affordances rather than remaining fixed by cultural convention. True conative needs, in other words, would have to be disentangled from cultural conventions and met with responsive flexibility.

This point may be elegantly rendered in Daoist terms. *Dao* is, according to the *Daodejing*, internalized in each individual living thing as *de*, the power or potentiality of that thing to manifest in accordance with Dao. In other words, while Dao denotes the intermeshed unfolding of things at the cosmological level in accordance with *li*, as we noted earlier, *de* denotes the power of a particular thing to unfold itself in accordance with Dao. The *de* of an individual is the form of its inclination when that inclination has been shaped, jigsaw-style, by reference to the specific environmental conditions that surround it. The core conative nature of the thing in question, as plant or animal, finds more specific form as it seeks self-articulation over time within the constraints of a particular environment. It fits itself to those constraints, in the way that a jigsaw piece fits itself to the surrounding puzzle. The *de* of forbs, or small herbaceous plants, that grow on mown areas like football fields, for example, is likely to be flat and spreading while the *de* of forbs that grow between large boulders will tend to be upright and tall. The *de* of the bettong is to dig for truffles. *De* is referenced to habitat but also to location. Our task as humans, released from instinctual ends and predetermined environments by our capacity for reflexivity, is to re-discover our own specifically human *de*. This is the task that Law sets us.

To approach the question of architecture from this perspective, then, is first to ask, metaphorically, what does the river want, in this connection? What does the river – or the local ecological community at large – need us to desire in respect of housing? A likely answer is that it would prefer us to do nothing at all – to make use of existing housing stock rather than tearing down and rebuilding. The twin principles of accommodation and least resistance are surely usually best met simply by repurposing whatever is already available – refurbishing, repairing, rearranging as needed, and in the process preserving the character, mnemonic richness, story and history of the place in question, 'letting the world grow old'.[7]

But if there are truly new housing or other architectural needs that cannot be met through repurposing existing housing and building stock, then we can look for a site that might benefit from synergizing with us. Are there species indigenous to that site, or to the surrounding area, that might be disposed to provide suitable materials for our use? Are there already ecological landscapers on hand such as termites or, in marine environments, coral polyps, that might appreciate frames or substrates afforded by us? Were such landscapers on hand, and were they to accept our invitation to fashion structures also habitable by us, those habitations would presumably look nothing like the houses to which we are accustomed. But were we able to adjust our expectations, not only would housing be provided for us relatively free from effort on our part, but our need for housing would open up opportunities for the

---

7 I discuss this attitude of 'affirming the given' as an aspect of the *wuwei* approach extensively in my 2005 book *Reinhabiting Reality*.

landscaping species in question as well as for the numerous other species that would inevitably colonize the resultant structures.

I am not yet aware of any examples of human housing built gratis in this way by nonhuman ecological landscapers, though there are certainly many examples of organisms colonizing artificial underwater structures, such as shipwrecks, pier pilings and concrete foundations of off-coast installations like wind farms as well as intentionally laid substrates for reef restoration (Ichioka and Pawlyn 2022). More tangible at present are the opportunities that architecture affords us to become ecological landscapers ourselves. One case in point is the astonishing architecture of the Marsh Arabs, or Ma'dan people, of Iraq, as described by Julia Watson in her book *Lo-TEK: Design by Radical Indigenism*. Situated in the vast Mesopotamian marshes, the unique civilization of the Ma'dan was based on floating islands and villages all woven entirely from the 8-metre-tall, bamboo-like Qasab reed that thrives in the marshes. Qasab provided not only the – fully biodegradable – materials for island construction and for the weaving of dwellings, religious centres, barns, fences and canoes but also flour for bread and fodder for domestic animals. The handmade dwellings of the Ma'dan were not only extraordinarily beautiful but could be woven in a matter of days, while the marshes themselves provided an ideal environment for husbanding water buffalo and growing rice. The floating Ma'dan structures returned benefits to the marshes, improving water quality and ensuring a rich diversity of habitat for species such as fish, turtles, snakes, frogs and a variety of birds (Watson 2020: 318). As Watson says, this example 'suggests a new trajectory for interdisciplinary indigenous innovation in which architecture and landscape architecture symbiotically grow the infrastructures of the future, in turn multiplying the ecosystem services embedded in our constructed environments' (308). Sadly, the marshes started to be drained in the 1950s; in the 1990s the Ma'dan were persecuted and driven out. But restoration is currently taking place and the area has been declared a World Heritage site by UNESCO.

For another example of architecture-as-ecological-landscaping, we can turn to Bali, to the traditional art of bamboo building, as discussed by Ichioka and Pawlyn in their book *Flourish: Design Paradigms for Our Planetary Emergency* (2022). Bamboo grows extremely rapidly so a thicket can soon establish itself and become a perennial ecosystem, a site of abundant opportunities for many species. A handmade dwelling woven from *in situ* bamboo may then be set within the thicket. Bamboo is non-standardized so the architect cannot work from a design blueprint. Instead, she starts with a miniature model woven from the very bamboo with which she will build. She then just upscales, using the natural curvature of bamboo to dictate the form of the structure. Bamboo, be it noted, is as strong as steel. The dwelling, which may be large and intricate or simple and small, may be regularly adapted and repaired as conditions and circumstances evolve.[8]

New building stock revisoned from a biosynergy perspective might depart even further from the monumental 'architecture of forever' tradition so beloved by the West in favour of more improvised and temporary modes. Such transient architecture might deploy fully biodegradable structures that could be erected and recycled as the need arose. Western readers might recoil from this suggestion, anticipating deep cultural loss from such a move away from stone, brick, concrete and steel towards an aesthetic of architectural transience. But as climate change increasingly undermines the possibility of permanence, the appeal of an aesthetic of transience might increase. As I write, large swathes of the eastern coast of Australia have succumbed to unprecedented floods. Thousands of homes have been submerged and people rescued from rooftops. Two years ago, many of the same areas were engulfed in unprecedented fires. For how long will it continue to make sense for us under these conditions to invest all our economic and personal resources in private houses intended to serve as our 'castle and fortress'? May not these conditions begin to shift our sense of place, identity and history away from monuments and built environments towards landscape itself, local landscapes which endure, even in the face of climate vicissitudes, and whose ecologies it may become our collective responsibility to nurture?

At the very least, we might take up the suggestion of architect, Frank Duffy, that buildings be designed for adaptation, with a permanent basic structure perhaps, such as foundations and frame, but with adjustable internal structures that may be dismantled, repurposed or recycled as the need arises (Ichioka and Pawlyn 2022: 81). This would surely represent a step away from the architecture of forever towards a new aesthetic of adaptive and responsive transience.

An acceptance of transience in relation to residence might move architecture closer to the Australian Aboriginal trope of the 'camp'. A traditional camp, as Alison Page and Paul Memmott explain in their book, *Building on Country*, is generally only minimally material – perhaps a bough shelter or wind break crafted from *in situ* vegetation together with a hearth from rocks. Such material simplicity in no way implies that camps are unsophisticated in their 'design' however but rather that their design is more a matter of protocol than of blueprint. To set up an overnight camp is to follow elaborate rules that relate not only to the selection of the site – with a view to shelter, comfortable

---

8 For examples, see https://www.ted.com/talks/elora_hardy_magical_houses_made _of_bamboo?language=en.

terrain and proximity to resources such as food plants and water – but to the social organization of the space. Kinship and avoidance relationships as well as totemic relationships with surrounding country must be observed in the lay-out of the camp. Such protocols extend moreover to how people should behave in camp: yarning around the campfire is not as informal as it may appear to a casual observer but is guided by responsibilities to rehearse – to memorialize – stories of the country in which the travellers are camped – stories of Songlines and Dreamings, for example, but also personal recollections of previous travel in the area. There are thus ceremonial aspects to the architecture of the camp as well socio-spatial aspects. The protocols are above all addressive – to set up camp is to address Country in a respectful and fully mindful manner, in anticipation of and gratitude for its kindness (Page and Memmott 2021). Summing up, Memmott points to the 'range of cognitive, invisible, ephemeral and symbolic properties [that] instil Aboriginal architecture with a culturally distinct nature' (Page and Memmott 2021: 126).

This may be a long way from received Western notions of architecture, but it conveys the core of Country-centred design – remembering that Country, in Aboriginal culture, is not so far removed from the idea of a living cosmos, when that cosmos is no longer equated with the physicist's cosmos conceived on a purely extensional plane. Country, as we will recall from Lecture 3, is sentient, communicative, always local, a potentially companionable and collaborative presence. Praxis, whether in architecture or in any other field of endeavour, is first and foremost addressed to this localized cosmos. As such, it must be essentially as communicative as it is beholden to Law, since Law and communicativity are, I suggested in Lecture 2, aspects of the living cosmos that cannot be separated: we only discover Law as Law, in the sense of falling under it, by feeling its communicative pull.

Turning now from architecture to the sphere of manufacture generally, is there any way that this sphere could conform to the protocol of biosynergy? Our first step in putting any prospective commodity to the biosynergy test would clearly be to ask the question, is the desire for this commodity one which, metaphorically speaking, the river, or more literally, the biosphere, needs us to want? Answering this question would rapidly lead us to discard many of those prospective commodities.[9] Nonetheless, even after the elimination of patently superfluous and injurious commodities, a multitude of legitimate human needs might remain for which biosynergic solutions cannot

---

9 The fashion industry springs instantly to mind in this connection, but so too does the chemicals industry, which has since the 1960s released 120,000 industrial and agricultural products, mostly without testing (Cribb 2014)).

yet be found. In the context of present-day market realities then, biosynergy might need to be compromised if these needs are to be satisfied. We might accordingly settle at this stage for the condition that (i) our manufacturing economy be based on living resources and production processes, and (ii) that these living resources and processes should be used in ways that enrich and enlarge ecosystems rather than degrading or destroying them.

Many plant-derived industrial materials are already under investigation. These include bamboo, as already mentioned, flax and mycelium. Kelp itself can be used in products such as soap and glass. One of the most promising industrial crops however is hemp. The fibre of industrial hemp is so versatile in its uses that a virtually hemp-based manufacturing sector seems conceivable. The 25,000 currently recognized commercial uses of hemp include high quality paper; biodegradable construction plastics; tough, antimicrobial clothing and fabric; carpets; a durable, fire- and pest-resistant building material (hempcrete) that continues to absorb CO_2 from the atmosphere even after installation; insulation; biofuels; as well as nutrient-rich foods (seeds, oil, flour and protein) and therapeutic products such as balms.[10] Many of these commodities might fail the biosynergy test and thus be ruled out. The technologies that would be needed to produce them might moreover in many instances fail the living-resources-only requirement. But the great number and variety of these commercial uses indicate the potential feasibility of a manufacturing sector based only on living resources.

As a crop, fast-growing hemp is lauded for its sustainability virtues: it draws down more carbon than any other broad-acre crop and its production is carbon-negative. It is largely self-fertilizing and requires no pesticides or herbicides. It is a soil remediator, drawing up heavy metals, and its deep roots – up to 9 metres long – help to hold soil together and prevent erosion. By replacing trees, which take decades to grow, as a source of pulp for paper products, hemp could largely replace forestry industries and thereby promote forest conservation. Hemp plantations moreover do not displace native forests, as do, say, palm oil plantations, since hemp can only be grown on the kinds of soils that are already in service to agriculture. On the deficit side, however, hemp is grown as a monoculture: hemp plantations seem not themselves to afford significant habitat for wildlife. But the possibility of cultivating hemp polycultures with high biodiversity values, or even using hemp in rewilding scenarios, remains as yet unexplored (Montford and Small 1999).

---

10 For a more comprehensive list of the environmental benefits and sustainable uses of hemp, see Ecological Agriculture Projects at McGill University: https://eap.mcgill.ca /CPH_3.htm

Whatever the living resources on which a new manufacturing sector may be based, the protocols for cultivating them will need to be sensitive to context. Indeed, whether in agriculture, manufacture, infrastructure or architecture, our praxical interventions must be responsive to specific ecological, geographical and indeed historico-cultural conditions and conceived consistently with them. At any scene of production, our interventions will start by accommodating 'the given', addressing the conativities and energies already at play and responding adaptively to them. Without such address, a strategic orientation, with its accompanying *wuwei* sensibilities, cannot be fostered.

A Concluding Chorus

In this book I have proposed that transition to an ecological civilization begins with an acknowledgement of Law. Law is understood as an existential protocol, an 'Ought' that is immanent in the very fabric of Creation and is already familiar to us from the testimony of pre-agrarian peoples. Law in this sense is grasped, under its normative aspect, only via strategic practice: it may be previewed in abstract via theory but can only be understood as binding, as Law, via interactivity in a field of inter-conative relations. As one articulation of this protocol, I have suggested the twin principles of conativity and accommodation/least resistance, principles that not only exceed the scientific picture of the universe but align with the Daoist notion of *wuwei*, or in more contemporary terminology, with the protocol of biosynergy.

This metaphysical 'Ought' at the core of the cosmic 'Is' seems at last to be coming into focus in our own time via the new, emerging paradigm of regenerativity. Pioneers of this paradigm in the design field, Pamela Mang and Bill Reed, describe how regenerative practitioners use their skills to foster 'the inherent creativity of the systems in which they are working' instead of viewing those systems as a palette for expressing their own creativity. Such practitioners see their task as being not to author, *in abstracto* and *ex situ*, 'things and structures in isolation from their context', but to design 'living systems with built-in evolutionary capacity' (Mang and Reed 2020: 30). Although retaining the vocabulary of design, so redolent of the blueprint model and hence of *theoria,* the regenerative paradigm is clearly pointing towards praxis as protocol-based rather than blueprint-based, and is hence aligned with biosynergy.

A growing number of contemporary thinkers are converging, from independent starting points, on core principles for a regenerative paradigm that could serve as axioms for a new ecological civilization. Julia Watson, as we have seen, looks to Indigenous praxes for inspiration, cleverly coining the term, lo-TEK, to describe traditional Indigenous infrastructures that 'are local, inexpensive, handmade, and easily constructed … [and that] amplify mutually beneficial interactions between multiple species' (Watson 2020: 21). She uses the term, *symbiosis,* to describe such interactions, and sees traditional praxes as the seed from which a new, symbiotic vision of design can take shape, a vision she describes as *radical indigenism.* From the perspective of radical indigenism, human praxis is 'an evolutionary extension of life in symbiosis with nature' (18).

Judith Schwartz curates case studies of nature-led agricultural and conservation praxes, illustrating how when ecosystems and wildlife are simply allowed to get on with the job of doing what they want to do, they can, sometimes with a helping hand from us, heal the damage that our brutal modern forms of praxis have inflicted. Pawlyn and Ichioka offer the term, co-evolutionary design, which they define as design which 'supports the flourishing of all life, for all time' (Ichioka and Pawlyn 2022: 114). The concept of design itself is reconceived by them as an inclusive, negotiated and co-creative process undertaken in collaboration with the human and other-than-human communities invested in the project (115). They too note the centrality of *symbiosis* to the idea of regenerativity, while remarking on an important distinction between two biological terms, *symbiosis* and *symbiogenesis,* a distinction clarified by renowned biologist Lynn Margulis. Symbiotic organisms cooperate with one another for their mutual but separately constituted advantage, while symbiogenesis refers to a relation between parties which is not only cooperative but also changes the constitution – or as I would put it, the conativity – of each party: the conativity of each is transformed and enlarged by its relation to the other. This is the relationship I have here termed biosynergy (Mathews 2006). Pawlyn and Ichioka stir different variants of the symbiotrope into the mix, enriching the emerging paradigm.

In his genre-busting book *Sand Talk,* written with all the wry subversiveness and humour of a contemporary Zhuangzi, Aboriginal cultural and design thinker Tyson Yunkaporta explores the relational ontology at the heart of Aboriginal knowledge. There is no way, he explains, that a relational system can be grasped from outside the system. It can always only be known from the unique, limited and local perspectives of its elements, since multi-perspectivalism is the driver of its self-organization. But a set of operating protocols does exist for the elements, protocols that we as elements need to observe if we wish to preserve the ongoing integrity of the system. These protocols are: connect, diversify, interact and adapt. Connection, diversification and interaction pertain to the enactment and increase of relationships, ensuring that elements do not become closed to the wider system, isolated and unchanging. One must share knowledge, energy and resources across widening networks, rather than trying to store them individually. The most important protocol, however, is adaptivity. 'You must allow yourself to be transformed through your interactions with other agents and the knowledge that passes through you to them. This knowledge and energy will flow through the entire energy system in feedback loops and you must be prepared to change so that those feedback loops are not blocked' (Yunkaporta 2020: 99). This chimes neatly with the symbio-trope.

In another recent book, *The Web of Meaning*, cultural theorist Jeremy Lent, whose project significantly parallels the one presented here, attempts to provide a philosophical frame for this same paradigm. He develops a basically fractal account of ethics: life consists in a systems-theoretic pattern of self-organization which is repeated holarchically at every level of system, from the cellular to the biospherical. It is to this holarchical order – in which each level represents a further iteration of the same root pattern or form of organization – that we of course owe our own existence. To find our specifically human form (or *de*, to put it into Daoist terms) we accordingly have to discover and fit ourselves to that root pattern, the pattern that is re-articulated at every systems-level of life. And what is this root pattern, but – symbiosis! (Lent 2021).

Philosopher Glenn Albrecht urges us to 'exit the Anthropocene and enter the Symbiocene'. He jettisons the concept of democracy, as irremediably anthropocentric, and proposes instead the term *sumbiocracy*, defined as 'political rule or governance committed to the types and totality of mutually beneficial or benign relationships in a given socio-biological system at all scales (mutualism)' (Albrecht and Van Horn 2016).

In all these treatments, the symbio-trope, or its counterparts, resonates strongly with the present notion of biosynergy, though biosynergy has a particular metaphysical genealogy and distinctive emphases. For many purposes, such differences do not matter: it is the convergence that is significant. But new paradigms can be quickly co-opted, as we have witnessed in the case of sustainability, and as we are possibly witnessing in the case of biomimicry discourse. To avoid regenerativity also being reduced to a few slogans ripe for co-optation, it may be important to keep the distinctive emphases of the various approaches in view. In the present case, these would include, firstly, that Law, as perceived through the lens of biosynergy, cannot be fully grasped, let alone have normative force, merely as discourse but needs to be discovered strategically, via practice – and hence, at a societal level, via praxis. The 'energy' embedded in the concept of biosynergy is not after all merely energy in the physicist's sense but is more akin to *qi*, the indwelling, truly holistic, psychophysical energy of conativity; if such energy is to be known at all, it must be experienced inwardly as well as observed outwardly by way of its empirical effects.

Secondly, biosynergy subsumes both conativity and accommodation/least resistance. As such it represents not merely an altruistic abnegation of self in favour of other but also a robust *increase* and *enlargement* of self. Synergy achieves, in other words, in good Daoist style, a kind of 'morality without morality': in sustaining others we assure our own best existence. The existential logic at the core of the synergic strategy – the logic of least resistance – also offers an intuitive short-cut to synergic solutions amidst the jumbled complexity of real-life circumstances.

Thirdly, let us recall that Law was not the only guide to aligning with a living cosmos: communicativity was also key. The living cosmos increases its existence inwardly by self-differentiating into a manifold of mutually communicative finite selves with whom it can share perspectives and thereby actualize and increase the field of intersubjective meaning. By acting in accordance with Law, we regenerate and increase this manifold of selves, while by engaging communicatively both amongst ourselves and with the cosmos itself, we co-create the field of meaning. In the context of the living cosmos, then, biosynergy calls not merely for ecological reciprocity but for ontopoetics, for poetic congress between selves and their world.

At a societal level, this means that economic praxis, reconfigured along biosynergy lines, would also comprise our major platform for poetic engagement with the cosmos. Through praxis we could establish synergy not only at a conative level but at a communicative level by adding invocational or ceremonial dimensions to our economic life. We might for example dedicate our installations to the elements or species to which they are referenced: the sea in the case of the kelp industry; the marshes in the case of reed-woven architecture; the sun in the case of any forms of solar power that might pass the biosynergy test. 'Industry' would become storied, acquiring intrinsic narrative and votive dimensions in addition to its functional one. By adding such poetic address to economic praxis, all members of society would become tuned to the larger cosmic context in which our economic life takes place.

Indeed, perhaps one day praxes could become vehicles of the great rituals of cosmic renewal traditionally performed in many pre-agrarian societies. In these rituals human beings cast themselves as co-creators of the cosmos, intuiting that human conativity and cosmo-conativity are not ultimately distinct but that the former can invigorate the latter and vice versa. Such rituals set up ceremonial synergies between humanity and cosmos.

Daoism itself offers one of the most impressive examples of this kind of ritual. According to Daoist scholar Martin Palmer, the main function of contemporary Daoist priests is 'that of ensuring the continued cycle of cosmic renewal liturgies. These try to make sure that the balance of yin and yang, the action between Heaven, Earth and Humanity, and the eternal struggle between order and chaos are kept going along the lines of the Way. ... these liturgies carry a basic message about the relationship between human beings and the rest of creation, both spiritual and material. The message is that the role we have to play is that of tending the balance and maintaining the harmony. If we fail to do this, then chaos and disorder break out on the Earth, and the world as we know it will collapse. It is within these vast, cosmic, liturgical and ritualistic roles that Humanity finds its true destiny according to Taoism' (Palmer 1991: 125–126).

Amen to that. The key to an ecological civilization from the perspective of a living cosmos is not so much the small-is-beautiful or minimal-is-best approach of earlier philosophies of sustainability, but synergy in a fully psychophysical sense. The aim is not to keep praxis as rudimentary as possible but to make it a vehicle of cosmic renewal. This may be achieved via large-scale interventions as well as via small-scale ones. As a vehicle of cosmic renewal such interventions will engage us communicatively with reality in the process of providing for our material needs. Praxis may thus be envisioned as eventually becoming our premier channel, at a societal level, for ontopoetics, its modifications of the landscape as at home in the annals of myth and story as were the windmills and waterwheels – and gentle, trickling, fires – of yesteryear.

EPILOGUE

What Does the Dragon Want?

Years ago, when I still used air transport, I was flying home from Canberra at sunset early one evening. I was gazing out the window as the plane passed over snow-powdered alps. The mountains stretched on and on to the curved horizon, unpeopled, the ribbon of a rare road showing up only now and then. The landscape was wrapped in pink haze, deepening to a glowing rose around the edges of the world, without any line at all between land and sky. I gazed and gazed, in nameless reverie. Feelings I could not identify moved in me, a sense that the presence I was forever seeking yet which remained just out of sight, just out of reach, was there. In my reverie I imagined that the wild vista on which I was gazing was populated by dragons and sages in caves – that mystery still dwelt down there. I imagined that I was separated from that mystery, or its larger source, only by an invisible veil. There lay the enchanted world, as real and beautiful as it could be, but I was looking at it from within the bubble of modernity, the aeroplane with its packaged food, plastic cups, glossy commercial magazines along with its cargo of trussed-up moderns.

Thinking about it today, I wonder if the question that architect, William McDonough, did not quite ask offers an opening through that veil: what do those mountains and the rivers running through them and the rosy fields of light in which they float want from us? Imagine the river-dragon slipping down from its alpine sources towards the sea, its tail trailing out into the Milky Way. Imagine it lifting its long neck and looking about as it streams along. It sees peaks and gullies sculpting the fields of energy through which it swims. There are tall trees and riparian groves and upland cress-fields and pastures drinking up dragon water and breathing out plumes of atmosphere, cascades of weather. Birds as bright as berries light up the woods, greeting one another from the little sanctuaries they have spun in the trees on the dragon's flanks. Furred creatures sleep and wake, climb and hop and yearn as the dragon passes. The dragon reaches out to all of them, finding in them new aspects of itself, new opportunities for self-differentiation into richer and more wakeful being. But now it slips into the lowlands, and as it peers over its banks it sees the hard lines of our freeways, it feels the shudder of our roadtrains, of our huge harvesters in its fields, our logging trucks in its forests. The towerblocks and smokestacks of our cities appear on its horizons, and soon intrude onto its very banks. The dragon sees my aeroplane in its skies. To its supernormal sensibilities, the stain of the aeroplane's poisonous wake is plainly visible. It sees our satellites amongst its stars. Observing all these things, what does it think? What does this great living, dreaming coil of slip-streaming energy that slithers along its path of least resistance and is nothing less, ultimately, than the core of reality itself, make of our hectic presence, our distracted activities, in its world? What are the opportunities that we represent for it? This is the question that our societies, seeking to reintegrate themselves into reality, must at last address. Having once conceded that reality is not merely physical but also psychoactive in its essential character, we realize that it has never been 'our' world at all, but belongs to itself. As part of that world, we belong to it. What is our role in the dragon's world?

Since the energy that courses around the landscape in dragon-veins is psychophysical and not merely physical in nature, this landscape is not only a theatre for physical process but for the birth of meaning. It is a theatre for poetics. And it is perhaps in our capacity to initiate poetic process with reality, our capacity to sing the dreaming dragon into poetic expression, that our special gift to Creation lies. Through the principles of ecology, reality has already perfected the process of life-differentiation and life-increase at the physical level, and our task, in that connection, is merely to take custody of that inter-conative process and nourish its integrity. But *inside* the world, in the terrain of interiority to which Indigenous peoples, such as Australian Aborigines and the Daoists of ancient China, have always had access, a whole new terrain of creative possibility opens. Is it perhaps in this realm that the task that is expected of us lies?

The dragon, long undisturbed in its fertile dreaming, is stirring now as rust-heaps of junk and avalanches of plastic clog its streaming and as strange new fluorescences corrode its flanks. It is craning its long neck to see far beyond its banks and it is asking itself, whose world is this anyway? It is watching crowds of 'consumers' rushing along the rat-runs they have constructed here, there and everywhere across the face of land and sea. And it is wondering how it can 'manage' them, how it can fit them into the enchanted lair, the vast cosmic corridors of poetic possibility, that are its world. It notices that they are blind, that they seem to see only the hard outer carapace of the landscape, that they charge right past the portals that open into its interiority, into the inner sanctums of the dragon's lair. If they cannot find their way into the poetic field of meaning that is the dragon's dreaming, what will the dragon do with them?

In the West the dragon became, long ago, a figure to be slain. This archetype of primal charge and tail-lashing motility, slipping along cosmic courses, its heedless incessancy the very essence of fertility, became, in the Western imagination, an opponent to be destroyed. In the formation of this opposition, the figure of the Hero was born: Western Man, spawned in mortal combat with the very force of life, intent on his mission of domination and control. A futile mission, since he who destroys life also dies. No wonder then that Western Man's gift to humanity, modernity, has brought environmental collapse in its train.

But there are alternatives. In China the dragon, as cosmic prototype but also as living and responsive presence, has always been an auspicious and revered figure. Respect has been reserved for those men and women who can win its trust and harness its inner-and-outer power – the immortals who mount the dragon and ride the white clouds. There is no Hero in Chinese mythology, no glorification of those who attain their ends by pitting themselves against circumstance in bone-headed displays of force. May China remember the secret of its dragon and join with other dragon-revering nations of Asia in a confederation that rests on the premise that our planet is first and foremost the dragon's world. And may Australia, where the dragon, as rainbow serpent, still roams wild and initiates those who seek it into the serpentine mysteries of *liyan*, join the dragon confederation. And may the countries of Europe remember their indigenous dragons, and call home their dragon-slayers, and appoint instead dragon-singers, environmental animateurs, who will convene gatherings of communities and educators, designers and artists and scientists to converse with local rivers, forests, swamps, oceans, birds and animals, to create cultures of richly recursive poetics and skilful praxes that will enact these poetics to the dragon's content. And may the other countries of the world follow suit, each cluster of countries forming their own regional confederations. From the dragon's viewpoint what distinguishes us, as peoples, is not our costumes and doctrines and prejudices but our varying sensitivities to the dragon's presence and to the question, what does the dragon want? When we are prepared to answer that question from the depths of an ecological and ontopoetic engagement with reality, we will indeed become one humanity, our cultures inter-cohering into a new civilization, a civilization shaped by the Law of the living cosmos itself.

ACKNOWLEDGEMENTS

The Letter in Part I appeared originally as

"On Greatness: A Philosopher's Letter to President Xi Jinping." *ABC Religion and Ethics*, 5 February 2021. https://www.abc.net.au/religion/greatness-a-philosophers-letter-to-president-xi-jinping/13126794.

Several modified passages from the following essays by the author appear in the book.

In Lectures 1 and 2:

"Law in the Living Cosmos: The "Ought" That is Core to the "Is"" (2021) in Joshua Farris and Benedikt P. Gocke (eds), *Routledge Handbook on Idealism and Immaterialism*, Routledge: London: 481–495.

In Lecture 3

"Conservation Needs to Include a "Story About Feeling"" (2022) *Biological Conservation*, 272, August
"Towards a Deeper Philosophy of Biomimicry" (2011a) *Organization and Environment*, 24, 4: 364–387.
"Why Has the West Failed to Embrace Panpsychism?" (2009) in David Skrbina (ed), *Mind That Abides: Panpsychism in the New Millennium*, John Benjamins: Philadelphia: 341–260.

The book also draws on a number of the author's other earlier works. Please refer to these works for more comprehensive coverage of the ideas as well as for further references.

"An Invitation to Ontopoetics: The Poetic Structure of Being" (2007) *Australian Humanities Review*, 43.
"Beyond Modernity and Tradition: Towards a Third Way for Development" (2006) *Ethics and the Environment*, 11, 2: 85–114.
"Biomimicry and the Problem of Praxis" (2019b) *Environmental Values*, 28: 573–599.
"Do the Deepest Roots of a Future Ecological Civilization Lie in Chinese Soil?" (2016) in John Makeham (ed), *Learning From the Other: Australian and Chinese Perspectives on*

Philosophy, Australian Academy of the Humanities and Chinese Academy of Social
    Sciences: Canberra: 15–27.
"Environmental Philosophy" (2015) in Nick Trakakis and Graham Oppie (eds), *A History
    of Philosophy in Australia and New Zealand*, Springer: Dordrecht: 543–591.
For Love of Matter: A Contemporary Panpsychism (2003) SUNY Press: Alberta.
"From Wilderness Preservation to the Fight for Lawlands" (2020) in Robyn Bartel, Marty
    Branagan, Fiona Utley, and Stephen Harris (eds), *Rethinking Wilderness and the Wild:
    Conflict, Conservation and Co-Existence*, Routledge: New York: 254–273.
"Living Cosmos Panpsychism" (2019a) in William Seager (ed), *Routledge Handbook on
    Panpsychism*, Routledge: London: 131–143.
"Moral Ambiguities in the Politics of Climate Change" (2011c) in Ved Nanda (ed), *Climate
    Change and Environmental Ethics*, Transaction Press: New Jersey.
"Panpsychism: Position Statement" and "First Response" (2017a) in Graham Oppy and
    Nicholas Trakakis (eds), *Inter-Religious Philosophical Dialogues*, Routledge: London: 45–
    71, 136–159.
"Panpsychism as Paradigm" (2011b) in Michael Blamauer (ed), *The Mental as Fundamental*,
    Ontos Verlag: Frankfurt.
Reinhabiting Reality: Towards a Recovery of Culture (2005) SUNY Press: Alberta.
"The Dilemma of Dualism" (2017b) in Sherilyn MacGregor (ed), *Routledge International
    Handbook on Gender and Environment*, Routledge: New York.
The Ecological Self (1991, 2021) Routledge: London.
"Thinking From Within the Calyx of Nature" (2008) *Environmental Values*, 17, 1: 41–65.

GENERAL BIBLIOGRAPHY

Doug Aberley (1999) "Interpreting Bioregionalism: A Story From Many Voices." in Michael McGinnis (ed), *Bioregionalism*. Routledge: London.

Glenn Albrecht and Gavin Van Horn (2016) "Exiting the Anthropocene and Entering the Symbiocene." May 24. https://humansandnature.org/exiting-the-anthropocene -and-entering-the-symbiocene.

Peter Andrews (2014) *Back From the Brink*, ABC Books: Sydney.

Gregory Bateson (1979) *Mind and Nature: A Necessary Unity*, Dutton: New York.

Gregory Bateson and Mary Catherine Bateson (1987) *Angels Fear: Towards an Epistemology of the Sacred*, Macmillan: New York.

Morris Berman (1981) *The Re-Enchantment of the World*, Cornell University Press: Ithaca.

Janine Benyus (2002) *Biomimicry: Innovation Inspired by Nature*, Harper Perennial: New York.

Martin Braungart and William McDonough (2002) *Cradle to Cradle: Remaking the Way We Make Things*, North Point Press: New York.

Henk Brinkhuis and Stefan Schouten (2006) "Episodic Fresh Surface Waters in the Eocene Arctic Ocean." *Nature*, 441: 606–609.

Christine Black (2011) *The Land is the Source of the Law: A Dialogical Encounter With Indigenous Jurisprudence*, Routledge-Cavendish: London.

Andrew Brennan and Norva Y. S. Lo (2021) "Environmental Ethics," in Edward N. Zalta (ed), *The Stanford Encyclopedia of Philosophy*. https://plato.stanford.edu/archives/ win2021/entries/ethics-environmental/.

Greg Campbell (2022) *Total Reset*, Total Reset Publishing: Dunsborough, WA. https:// totalreset.com.au.

David J. Chalmers (1996) *The Conscious Mind*, Oxford University Press: Oxford.

David Chalmers (2016) "The Combination Problem for Panpsychism," in Godehard Bruntrup and Ludwig Jaskolla (eds), *Panpsychism*, Oxford University Press: Oxford.

Alan Chan (2019) "Neo-Daoism," in Edward N. Zalta (ed), *The Stanford Encyclopedia of Philosophy (Summer Edition)*. https://plato.stanford.edu/archives/sum2019/entries/neo -daoism/.

Noel Charlton (2008) *Understanding Gregory Bateson: Mind, Beauty and the Sacred Earth*, SUNY Press: Albany New York.

Diana Coole and Samantha Frost (eds) (2010) *New Materialisms: Ontology Agency and Politics*, Duke University Press: Durham, NC.

Julian Cribb (2014) *Poisoned Planet: How Constant Exposure to Man-Made Chemicals is Putting Your Life at Risk*, Allen and Unwin: Sydney.

Eileen Crist (2019) *Abundant Earth: Toward an Ecological Civilization*. University of Chicago Press: Chicago.

Brian Easlea (1973) *Liberation and the Aims of Science*, Chatto and Windus: London.

Mark Elvin (2004) *Retreat of the Elephants: An Environmental History of China*, Yale University Press: New Haven.

Warwick Fox (1990) *Towards a Transpersonal Ecology: Developing New Foundations for Environmentalism*, Shambhala: Boston.

Tim Flannery (2017) *Sunlight and Seaweed*, Text: Melbourne.

Trish Fleming (2013) "Losing Australia's Diggers is Hurting Our Ecosystems." *The Conversation (Australia)*, September 25.

Bill Gammage (2011) *The Biggest Estate on Earth: How Aborigines Made Australia*, Allen and Unwin: Crow's Nest, NSW.

Phillip Goff (2019) *Galileo's Error: Foundations for a New Science of Consciousness*, Rider: London.

Ben Goldfarb (2018) "Beavers Are the Ultimate Ecosystem Engineers." *Sierra: The Magazine of the Sierra Club*, 3 July. https://www.sierraclub.org/sierra/2018-4-july -august/feature/beavers-are-ultimate-ecosystem-engineers.

David Graeber and David Wengrow (2021) *The Dawn of Everything: A New History of Humanity*, Penguin/Allen Lane: London.

Mary Graham (2019) "A Relationist Ethos: Aboriginal Law and Ethics." *Earth Ethics*, 1: 1–6.

Matthew Hall (2011) *Plants as Persons: A Philosophical Botany*, SUNY Press: Albany, NY.

Sam Hamill and J. P. Seaton (1999) *The Essential Zhuangzi*, Shambhala: Boston.

Graham Harvey (2012) "An Animist Manifesto." *PAN Philosophy Activism Nature*, 9: 2–4.

Tze-Ki Hon (2019) "Chinese Philosophy of Change (Yijing)," in Edward N. Zalta (ed), *The Stanford Encyclopedia of Philosophy* (Summer Edition).https://plato.stanford.edu/ entries/chinese-change/.

Sarah Ichioka and Michael Pawlyn (2022) *Flourish: Design Systems for Our Planetary Emergency*, Triarchy: Dorset, UK.

Alison Jaggar (1984) *Feminist Politics and Human Nature*, Harvester: Brighton.

Francois Jullien (2002) "Did Philosophers Have to become Fixated on Truth?" *Critical Inquiry*, 28, 4: 803–824.

Franklin Hiram King (2004) *Farmers of Forty Centuries: or Permanent Agriculture in China, Korea and Japan*. Originally Published in 1911; Republished in 2004 by Dover: New York.

Livia Kohn (2017) *Pristine Affluence: Daoist Roots in the Stone Age*, Three Pines: St Petersburg.

Michal Kravcik, J. Pokorný, J. Kohutiar, M. Kovác, and E. Tóth (2007) *Water for the Recovery of the Climate: A New Water Paradigm*, Krupa Print: Žilina.

Jacqueline Kurio and Peter Reason (2021) "Voicing Rivers Through Ontopoetics: A Co-Operative Inquiry." *River Research and Applications*, 1–9. https://doi.org/10.1002/ rra.3817.

Michael Lafargue (1992) *The Tao of the Tao Te Ching: A Translation and Commentary*, State University of New York Press: Albany.

Jeremy Lent (2017) *The Patterning Instinct*, Prometheus: New York.

Jeremy Lent (2021) *The Web of Meaning*, New Society: Gabriola, BC.

Melissa Lucashenko (2013) "They Used to be the 'Happiest People on the Earth." *The Drum, ABC*, 13 February.

Luisa Maffi (2010) *Biocultural Diversity Conservation: A Global Sourcebook*, Routledge: London.

Alex C. Maisey, Angie Haslem, Steven W. J. Leonard, and Andrew F. Bennett (2021) "Foraging by an Avian Ecosystem Engineer." *Ecological Applications*, 31: 1.

Pamela Mang and Bill Reed (2020) "Regenerative Development and Design: a Framework for Evolving Sustainability," Accessed via https://www.researchgate.net/publication/346075346_Regenerative_Development_and_Design.

Charles Massy (2017) *Call of the Reed Warbler: a New Agriculture, a New Earth*, University of Queensland Press: St Lucia.

William McDonough and Michael Braungart (2002) *Cradle to Cradle: Remaking the Way We Make Things*, North Point Press: New York.

Michael V. McGinnis (ed) (1999) *Bioregionalism*, Routledge: London.

Caroline Merchant (1980) *The Death of Nature*, Harper and Row: New York.

S. Montford and E. A. Small (1999) "A Comparison of the Biodiversity Friendliness of Crops With Special Reference to Hemp." *Journal of International Hemp Association*, 6: 53–63.

Arne Naess (1973) "The Shallow and the Deep, Long-Range Ecology Movement." *Inquiry* 16: 95–100.

Arne Naess (1885) "Identification as a Source of Deep Ecological Attitudes," in Michael Tobias (ed), *Deep Ecology*, Avant Books: San Diego.

Yujin Nagasawa and Khai Wager (2016) "Panpsychism and Priority Cosmopsychism," in Godehard Bruntrup and Ludwig Jaskolla (eds), *Panpsychism*, Oxford University Press: Oxford.

Eric S. Nelson (2021) *Daoism and Environmental Philosophy*, Routledge: New York.

Max Oelschlaeger (1991) *The Idea of Wilderness*, Yale University Press: New York.

Martin Palmer (1991) *The Elements of Taoism*, Element: Shaftesbury Dorset.

Bruce Pascoe (2014) *Dark Emu Black Seeds: Agriculture or Accident?* Magabala: Broome.

Alison Page and Paul Memmott (2021) *Design: Building on Country*, Thames and Hudson: London.

Val Plumwood (1993) *Feminism and the Mastery of Nature*, Routledge: London.

Michael Pollan (2013) "The Intelligent Plant." *The New Yorker*, December 15. https://www.newyorker.com/magazine/2013/12/23/the-intelligent-plant.

Anne Poelina, Sandra Wooltorton, Sandra Harben, Len Collard, Pierre Horwitz, and David Palmer (2020) "Feeling and Hearing Country." *PAN Philosophy Activism Nature*, 15, 6–15.

Anne Poelina, Sandra Wooltorton, Sandra Harben, Len Collard, Pierre Horwitz, and David Palmer (2021) "Hearing, Voicing and Healing: Rivers as Culturally Located and Connected." *River Research Applications*, 1–13.

Tom Regan (1983) *The Case for Animal Rights*, University of California Press: Berkeley.

Deborah Bird Rose (1992) *Dingo Makes Us Human*, Cambridge University Press: Cambridge.

Deborah Bird Rose (1996) *Nourishing Terrains: Australian Aboriginal Views of Landscape and Wilderness*, Australian Heritage Commission: Canberra.

Richard Routley (1973) "Is There a Need For New, an Environmental, Ethic?" *Proceedings of the 15th World Congress of Philosophy*, 1: 205–210.

Kirkpatrick Sale (1985) *Dwellers in the Land: The Bioregional Vision*, Sierra Club Books: San Francisco.

Allan Savory and Jody Butterfield (2017) *Holistic Management*, Island Press: Washington, DC.

Judith Schwartz (2020) *The Reindeer Chronicles*, Chelsea Green: Vermont.

Judith Schwartz (2013) *Cows Save the Planet*, Chelsea Green: Vermont.

Itay Shani (2015) "Cosmopsychism: A Holistic Approach to the Metaphysics of Experience." *Philosophical Papers*, 44, 3: 389–437.

Peter Singer (1975) *Animal Liberation*, New York Review: New York.

David Skrbina (2005) *Panpsychism in the West*, MIT Press: Cambridge, MA.

Nathan Sivin (1982) "Why the Scientific Revolution Did Not Take Place in China—Or Didn't It?" *Chinese Science*, 5: 45–66.

Jim Sinatra and Phin Murphy (1999) *Listen to the People, Listen to the Land*, Melbourne University Press: Melbourne.

Gary Snyder (2013) "Reinhabitation." *Manoa*, 25, 1: 44–48.

Judith D. Soule and Jon K. Piper (1992) *Farming in Nature's Image*, Island Press: Washington, DC.

Victor Steffensen (2020) *Fire Country*, Hardie Grant: Melbourne.

Eduardo Viveiros de Castro (1998) "Cosmological Deixis and Amerindian Perspectivism." *The Journal of the Royal Anthropological Institute*, 4, 3: 469–488.

Irene Watson (2000) "Kaldowinyeri Munaintya in the beginning." *Flinders Journal of Law Reform*, 4, 4: 1–6

Irene Watson (2014) *Aboriginal Peoples, Colonialism and International Law: Raw Law*, Routledge: London.

Julia Watson (2020) *Lo-TEK: Design by Radical Indigenism*, Taschen: Cologne.

Jonathan Watts (2010) *When a Billion Chinese Jump*, Simon and Schuster: New York.

Lynn White Jr (1967) "The Historical Roots of Our Ecological Crisis." *Science*, 155.

Richard Wilhelm (translator) (1964) *I Ching*, Arkana: London.

Edward O. Wilson and Bert Holldobler (2009) *The Superorganism*, W. W. Norton: New York.

Peter Wohlleben (2015) *The Hidden Life of Trees*, Ludwig Verlag: Munich.

Sandra Wooltorton, Anne Poelina, Len Collard, Pierre Horwitz, Sandra Harben, and David Palmer (2020a) "Becoming Family With Place." *Resurgence*, 322.

Sandra Wooltorton, Pierre Horwitz, Len Collard, and Anne Poelina (2020b) "Sharing a Place-Based Indigenous Methodology and Learnings." *Environmental Education Research*, 26, 1: 1–18.

Tyson Yunkaporta (2020) *Sand Talk*, Text: Melbourne.

INDEX